Anna Jones is a cook, food writer and stylist. She worked for many years as part of Jamie Oliver's food team – styling, writing and working behind the scenes on books, TV shows and food campaigns – and went on to work with some of the UK's biggest food brands and best-known chefs. She is the author of *A Modern Way to Eat*, widely acclaimed as a book of the year. *A Modern Way to Cook* is her second book. She lives, writes and cooks in Hackney, east London.

For Laura.
How lucky I am to have been put here
with you as my sister.

ANNA JONES

a modern way to cook

**Over 150 quick, smart and
flavour-packed recipes for every day**

Fourth Estate · *London*

Fourth Estate
An imprint of HarperCollinsPublishers
1 London Bridge Street
London SE1 9GF
www.4thestate.co.uk

First published in Great Britain by Fourth Estate in 2015

Text copyright © Anna Jones 2015
All photographs by Matt Russell except images on pages
22, 54, 102, 148, 224, 278, 304
Designed by Sandra Zellmer

Anna Jones asserts the moral right to be identified as the
author of this work

A catalogue record for this book is available from the
British Library

ISBN: 978-0-00-812449-6

All rights reserved. No part of this publication may be
reproduced, transmitted, or stored in a retrieval system,
in any form or by any means, without permission in
writing from Fourth Estate

MIX
Paper from
responsible sources
FSC® C007454

FSC
www.fsc.org

FSC is a non-profit international organisation established
to promote the responsible management of the world's
forests. Products carrying the FSC label are independently
certified to assure consumers that they come from forests
that are managed to meet the social, economic and
ecological needs of present and future generations, and
other controlled sources.

Find out more about HarperCollins and the environment
at www.harpercollins.co.uk/green

Printed and bound in Italy by L.E.G.O.

a modern way to cook

I'll make you some promises about the food in this book:

- **It's delicious, everyday food that will always be ready in a life-friendly time.**

- **All the recipes are packed with tricks to help you be smarter in the kitchen.**

- **The recipes are full of fantastic ingredients that will leave you feeling great.**

- **You will make amazing vegetables the focus of your meals as you eat through the seasons.**

- **And my hope is that, over time, these recipes will make you more aware of what you put into your body in the same way they have for me.**

Food for me is a celebration: three opportunities a day to sit, share and revel in nourishing myself and others with amazing ingredients. Being in my kitchen allows me to connect with far-flung locations I have travelled; it firmly roots me in the time, place and season when I see the blood oranges arrive just after Christmas or the wild garlic herald the first days of spring. It's these things that inform my cooking, day in, day out.

But I'm just the same as the next person. For all of us, our lives are busier than they have ever been. We have access to so much, and the world is at our fingertips like never before. While this is brilliant in many ways, it also comes with the temptation to try and fit even more into already jam-packed lives.

I have been overwhelmed by the positive response to my first book, *A Modern Way to Eat.* The world of social media has allowed me to be directly in contact with the wonderful people who have been cooking from it, and I've noticed that the stuff they've been getting excited about hasn't been the fancy cakes or showy dinners but the easy weeknight recipes, which have been cooked again and again.

From what I have seen, there is a sense that people are more energised about cooking – we are reaping the benefits of home-cooked, vegetable-focused food. We have more connection to what we are eating, and our relationship to what we eat seems to be becoming more balanced. Also we feel genuinely happy and excited about the food we are putting on our tables. It's proof to me that food is a powerful force for change and that what we eat can completely transform our outlook on life. The emails I receive on a weekly basis are evidence that there is a huge wave of change happening, which is an incredible thing.

From my experience working in homes, schools and kitchens, with kids, adults, parents and dinner ladies, I know for a fact that sitting down to a nourishing home-cooked meal every day can have a massive impact on our minds, bodies and overall happiness. It shouldn't just be something we do on a Sunday lunchtime or once in a blue moon. Cooking a home-made meal is the single most important thing we can do for our well-being, because then we know exactly what is going into our bodies. It allows us to honour the people we are cooking it for and it means that we also get a chance to sit round a table, eat, drink and really spend time with one another.

The more I cook simply – easy pastas, quick hearty salads and all-in-one gratins – the more I realise that food doesn't need to be posh, complicated or made from far-flung ingredients to do us good. It's the quick-to-make, everyday and weeknight meals that we eat on, say,

Tuesdays and Wednesdays that make a real difference in our lives. These meals are the 'bread and butter' of our eating week and the most important ones to focus on.

At the same time that we are being busier than ever, there is also a movement towards balancing things out. There's a desire to treat our bodies well and to look after ourselves physically, mentally and spiritually. And an awful lot of this centres around the food we eat.

There has been a real shift in the way we look at food. More people are conscious of what they're putting into their shopping baskets, more people are buying seasonally, and more people are cooking at home. For the first time in two generations, home cooking is firmly back in fashion and an ever-increasing number of people are actively choosing to eat a diet centred around vegetables on at least a few days a week.

Making vegetables the focus of our diet is widely considered to be the single most important thing we can do for our own health and for the health of the planet. Over the last couple of years, eating a plant-based diet has moved from the domain of brightly painted veggie cafés to proud centre stage.

I hope this book will show you how to do this in your home without too much fuss. It's packed full of the food I like to eat and the food I like to cook. To my mind, it's this straight-up everyday food that is so important for us to get right, and get enthused about. And it's the recipes in this book that I hope will help you cook achievable amazing meals every night of the week.

This book is my notebook of recipes, over 150 of them, flavour-packed with layers of texture and goodness. I hope they will be able to revolutionise how you cook and eat in the same way they have in my home. It's modern cooking, making the most

of a rainbow of grains and vegetables and using flavour and texture to transform your dinners into quick and easy feasts.

They're recipes I am really proud of. From super-clever and ridiculously quick fifteen-minute one-pot pasta, to a Buddha bowl curry feast that would be grand enough to grace any table, this is the food that makes me happy. The sort that drives my cooking, led by flavour, texture and a deep love and respect for food.

Eating well

I am passionate about eating food that makes me feel good, and while I'll sometimes reach for a trashy chocolate bar or a stodgy pub roast (which is all part of being human and nothing to be ashamed of), I know that's not the food that I feel good eating.

I want stand-out, delicious food that leaves me feeling energised, light, bright and satisfied. It's this intersection between wellness and deliciousness that I strive for with every plate of food I make and eat. And with all the talk of health and wellness in the food industry, I think this sweet spot is becoming ever more important. Wellness doesn't come at the expense of deliciousness.

I welcome with open arms the new breadth of information and attention around eating well, and I am so thrilled that we are all putting more focus on what we put into our bodies and on the connection between the food we eat and how vibrantly we live.

But I also think it's important to remember that we are all individuals, each with our own completely separate nutritional needs. I can tell you what works for my body, but I honestly can't tell you exactly what's going to work for yours. Nor in my opinion can any chef or, really, any nutritionist. While nutritionists can absolutely be a guide, it is you who have to do the work. You need to have a relationship with your body and a responsibility to listen to it and how it reacts to certain foods. If you feel tired and bloated after eating something, make a change next time – eat a smaller portion, or try a different way of cooking, or another ingredient.

There are lots of people out there ready to name superfoods that can help us lose weight, cure illness and make us more attractive and amazing. It sometimes feels to me as though all this sometimes over-the-top focus on nutrition and 'clean eating'

has almost become the new, more acceptable way to be on a diet. And in a weird way, that isn't promoting a healthy attitude to food at all.

It's important to make a commitment to eating well, but it's also important to be realistic. Cooking goodness-packed meals every night is going to have a huge impact on your health, and simply getting more vegetables into your diet is a great first step. You can worry about matcha and chia seeds later on.

To me, eating well is far more simple than it is often made out to be. Buy good ingredients, cook at home, make the majority of what you eat plants and vegetables, and listen and react to your body. I don't think it's much more complicated than that. Right now, too many sweeping generalisations are being made in the world of food. Foods like bread are being vilified, and chefs and nutritionists are making blanket statements about how certain staple, cheap and useful nutritious foods are unduly bad for our bodies. I think this is damaging, as it means our psychology around these foods changes. We attach guilt and a 'forbidden' label to food, increasing our anxiety around it and causing us to crave it even more.

My point here is this: let's stop looking at food in its respective parts, and making some bad and some disproportionately good. Let's get back to the whole picture, the whole food. Choosing a balanced way of eating and sticking as close to nature as we possibly can is the most realistic plan for eating long-term. Going to extremes is not a sustainable way of eating or living. What I am proposing here and with the recipes in this book is a sensible, flexible dietary strategy that we can incorporate into our lives successfully and joyfully, day-to-day, and over a lifetime.

The practice of quick, calm cooking

At home, I cook under the same constraints as anyone else. Even though I have a food background, when I come home from a day at work, feeling sometimes jaded with food, the last thing I want to do is spend hours at the stove. I am impatient, usually hungry, and I relish the art of cooking quickly. And that's what I want to share with you in this book. The clever secrets that chefs and cooks use, quick ways of cooking, smart cheats and ways of working logically which have your dinner on the table in a friendly and achievable time. All of this can happen in a calm and well-choreographed manner that won't leave your kitchen looking like a bombsite and having used every pan in the cupboard.

I know these recipes can come together in life-friendly times. I asked a kind band of brilliant friends, who aren't cooks, to test and time themselves, so I know they are achievable for everyone.

The recipes which take 15 minutes are quick supper recipes, delicious and simple, with just a few ingredients that come together in one pan without much chopping or fuss. The recipes that are ready in 20–30 minutes are a little more advanced, with more complex layers of flavour and texture and a few more ingredients, while those that take 40 minutes are real feasts, riots of flavour and colour that I would happily eat at any restaurant table.

In addition to these chapters, this books pivots around a chapter full of what I like to call investment cooking. It's batch cooking that you can do once a week, or even once a month in some cases, which will mean you have a freezer or fridge full of nourishing, cheap, home-cooked beans, snacks, grains and treats. It's this cooking that is the backbone of how I cook these days – a little time

one day a week yields enough chickpeas for a week's worth of stews and hummus, and they taste so much better. I find this type of cooking so satisfying, knowing for example that I have a homemade sweet treat to snack on when I hit a low at 4 p.m. rather than reaching for a biscuit.

There is also a chapter on my quick desserts and sweet treats, such as a 10-minute frying-pan crumble, as well as some really easy breakfasts that will make great starts to the day – interesting flavours that come together quickly and make the most of my favourite meal.

This way of cooking is all about simplifying the process, and to some of you that might sound really obvious. More often than not, when I ask people why a recipe hasn't worked, they reply that they burnt the onions while they were digging out the coriander seeds from the back of the cupboard, or something along these lines. The only way to cook speedy dinners and stay calm is to be organised upfront. I am sure all my friends will read this and laugh, as I have a reputation for being less than well-organised, but in the kitchen I am like a general. The kitchen is my realm and I know that the only way I can cook speedily is to be ordered, organised and calm, and work through the flow of jobs.

I think of cooking in this way as a practice. It's organised, calm and has a flow. It's not speedy, hectic, cheffy stuff. It's just about getting things right, so that you can enjoy every brilliant moment of the alchemy that happens as you turn a pile of ingredients into an incredible offering for you and your family.

So your kitchen needs to be ready to cook in this way. By this, I don't mean you have to buy loads

of expensive equipment. You just need to have an artillery of simple equipment which is accessible (see pages 20–1).

I find it really useful to have my ingredients organised too, so that I can find them easily and so that getting ready to cook doesn't mean half an hour emptying out the entire spice cupboard. I use little glass jars for my spices and keep them on a shelf within reach of the cooker, which makes things a lot simpler.

You'll also need a bit of space to cook in. My kitchen counters, like most other people's, can get cluttered, so before I settle down to cook something, I make sure I clear enough space to comfortably cook in. There are a few bits of equipment that can really help speed things up. You'll be fine if you just have the basics, but if you are, for instance, a particularly slow chopper, a food processor will be a great addition to your kitchen. Equally, if you find things keep sticking or burning, maybe it's time for some new pans. All this equipment is a massive investment in cooking from scratch, and that's the best decision we can make for our happiness and our bodies.

When you are ready to cook, start by reading the recipe from top to bottom so that you know what happens when, and how things need to be chopped and cooked. Then put all the equipment you are going to need close by, and get all your ingredients together near your chopping board so that you have everything to hand before you start chopping. These steps are the key to quick, calm cooking and they may sound glaringly obvious, but I have to remind myself to do them every time I cook.

Other clever chef's tricks that make my cooking more speedy are having a mixing bowl on the work surface for peelings and trimmings, so you don't have to keep running back and forth to the bin, as well as making sure as much as possible that the area you are working in is close to the stove, so you can do a few jobs at once.

I'm going to ask you to cook on a high heat, but don't be afraid of it. Just keep checking. I am also going to ask you to preheat your pans to get some serious heat on things that need it, and to speed things up with your kettle. It's my best friend in the kitchen, and working with boiling water rather than cold from the tap makes everything that bit quicker.

This might all sound somewhat hectic, but I believe that making these changes in your kitchen will actually have the opposite effect. You will learn to cook in a way that is calm and choreographed, moving quickly but smoothly through recipes.

And that's what cooking is for me – food that is flavour-packed, nourishing and not too fussy, that can be on your table in a life-friendly time and manner. It's about using the time you have, however short, to make the tastiest and most delicious dinners possible, and, in making the most of your time, the incredible ingredients that are in season and the foods that make you feel good, you can live vibrantly and eat well.

annajones.co.uk
@we_are_food

Equipment
for quick cooking

There are a few pieces of equipment I rely on in the kitchen. They range from really cheap to a bit more expensive, but once you have invested in a few of them you'll be able to make anything in a life-friendly time.

SPEED AND JULIENNE PEELERS   My speed peeler has to be the most used gadget in my kitchen and the cheapest. I use it for peeling and for making vegetable ribbons for salads and noodles. I also use a julienne peeler to make noodles from vegetables such as courgettes, it does the job of the currently popular spiraliser but costs about £2 and takes up much less kitchen space. My favourites are the all-metal ones from Lakeland.

GOOD FRYING PANS   A good frying pan will last a lifetime. I have a good non-stick pan in two sizes, 22cm and 26cm, as well as a heavy cast-iron frying pan and a griddle pan. My favourites are GreenPan (who use a non-toxic ceramic coating) and De Buyer.

A LARGE SAUCEPAN/STOCKPOT   I make a vat of soup, stock or a big pan of chickpeas every week and a large pot makes things much easier. It need not be expensive but it will allow you to cook batches big enough to last a week or fill the freezer. A heavy-bottom cast-iron pan would be my choice, from Le Creuset, but any sturdy large pan will do.

STACKABLE GLASS JARS   One of the things that makes a huge difference in my kitchen is having everything accessible and easy to find. I stack all my spices in small glass jars on a shelf next to my cooker, which means they are always at hand. I also keep my dry ingredients in large jars for easy access.

GRATERS – BOX GRATER AND FINE MICROPLANE
I use these every day. A good sturdy box grater should set you back between £5 and £10 and is great for grating cheese and vegetables. Microplanes are more cheffy graters and a bit more expensive but one will last a lifetime and they are invaluable for zesting citrus and finely grating garlic, chilli, ginger or any hard cheese.

GOOD KNIVES AND A GOOD KNIFE SHARPENER
The main barrier to cooking quickly is being a slow chopper – how good you are at chopping is directly related to how good and sharp your knives are. I use four main knives in the kitchen: a small chef's knife (about 12cm), a small serrated paring knife (for tomatoes and fruit), a larger chef's knife (about 21cm) for sturdy vegetables such as pumpkin or squash and a good serrated bread knife. I also have a sharpening stone to keep them nice and sharp. My favourite knives are Kin knives which aren't the cheapest but, equally, you can find knives that are much more expensive. They stay nice and sharp and last a lifetime. I like Opinel for small serrated paring knives, which are very affordable.

HIGH-SPEED BLENDER   I use my blender every day for smoothies, soups, nut butters and hummus. The king of blenders is the Vitamix, which has a super high-speed motor and will make nuts into butter in a matter of seconds. They are very expensive though, so I am not going to suggest you all run out and buy one, but they are a great investment if you spend a lot of time in the kitchen. Alternatively, most electrical brands make good sturdy blenders at varying prices – go for the best you can afford.

FOOD PROCESSOR   It may seem overkill to have a food processor and a blender but they really do different jobs. A blender will liquidise things whereas a food processor will chop and crush things and, if you buy one with some attachments, they can grate and slice too, as well as mixing up icings and cake batters. If I can encourage you to buy one thing for your kitchen it would be a food processor. I have had my Magimix for the last 12 years and it's still going strong. Magimix are great as they have a good range of attachments and are really sturdy, but other brands such as KitchenAid make good ones too. Again you get what you pay for here; I would suggest investing as much as you can afford.

HAND BLENDER   If you can't get your hands on a blender or a food processor, or your kitchen is too small for big pieces of equipment, then a decent hand blender will stand in for most things. You will need a bit more elbow grease and probably patience but it will do the job. I use my hand blender for making dressings and quick pestos and for blending soups, and I find it really useful. Hand blenders come pretty cheap and I use a basic £10 one which has been with me for years.

KITCHEN SCISSORS   A good sharp pair of kitchen scissors are always at hand in my kitchen for opening packets and doing little jobs. If you aren't the fastest at chopping with a knife, then chopping small things like herbs or spring onions can be done pretty quickly with a pair of scissors.

A few notes on ingredients

COCONUT OIL   I use coconut oil, which has a mild flavour and a higher smoking point than many other oils, so less nutrients are damaged when it's heated. I recommend coconut oil in many of the recipes in this book. If it's not for you though, you can generally use a plain olive oil in its place.

EXTRA VIRGIN GHEE   I use ghee (clarified butter) in place of butter. It's basically butter without the whey and full of nutrients such as vitamins A, D, E and K. It has a high smoking point, keeps for months and tastes amazing.

OLIVE OIL   I keep two types in my kitchen. One plain for gentle frying and a flavour-packed extra virgin for dressing and finishing – this NEVER sees the heat as it has a low smoking point and creates harmful free radicals if heated too high.

EGGS   The eggs I use throughout the recipes are medium eggs and I always use free range and organic eggs. If you are vegan in most of the baking in this book eggs can be replaced with 1 tablespoon of chia seeds mixed with 3 tablespoons of water, it should be set aside until it forms a gel.

SALT   I use British flaked sea salt – my favourite is Halen Môn from Anglesey which has a Protected Designation of Origin status so you know it's water from Wales (not imported salt re-diluted).

SWEET STUFF   I keep several natural sweeteners on hand. It is important to remember that while higher in nutrients than regular sugar all of these are sugars so should be used sparingly. Natural sweeteners do tend to be more expensive so you may want to go for one at a time. I keep these on rotation in my house: maple syrup, honey, agave, coconut sugar, coconut nectar.

CONGRATULATIONS.

in the
time
it takes
to set
the table

These recipes are for the days and nights when time is shortest and hunger is at its highest. We can all spare fifteen minutes to get dinner on the table. These are ready in the time it takes for the table to be set and are packed with flavour. Killer one-pot pastas, quick salads, herb-stuffed omelettes, brightly coloured speedy soups, piled-high sandwiches and super-easy quesadillas.

Kale, tomato and lemon magic one-pot spaghetti

This pasta is a complete revelation. The sauce is magically made from the pasta water and tomatoes as the pasta cooks all in one pan. No fuss, one pan and a killer bowl of pasta.

Pasta and gluten sometimes get a bad press. I think there is a time and place for a good bowl of pasta, saying that, I opt for interesting pastas as often as I do the traditional kind. Try corn, chickpea or buckwheat spaghetti – they are gluten-free, all have incredible individual flavours and make a welcome change if pasta is a staple in your house.

The key to this recipe is to measure your water carefully and to use the right pan: you need a large shallow sauté pan or a casserole large enough to fit the pasta lying down. A large deep frying pan or wok would work well too.

Fill and boil a kettle and get all your ingredients and equipment together. You need a large shallow pan with a lid.

Put the pasta into the pan. Quickly and roughly chop the tomatoes in half and throw them into the pan. Grate in the zest of both lemons and add the oil and salt. Add 1 litre of boiling water, put a lid on the pan and bring to the boil. As soon as it comes to the boil, remove the lid and simmer on a high heat for 6 minutes, using a pair of tongs to turn the pasta every 30 seconds or so as it cooks.

Meanwhile, remove any tough stalks from the kale or spinach and roughly tear the leaves. Once the pasta has had 6 minutes, add the kale and continue to cook for a further 2 minutes.

Once almost all the water has evaporated, take the pan off the heat and tangle into four bowls. If you like, top with a little Parmesan.

SERVES 4 GENEROUSLY

400g spaghetti or linguine

400g cherry tomatoes

the zest of 2 large unwaxed lemons

100ml olive oil

2 heaped teaspoons sea salt (if you are using fine-grain table salt, add a bit less)

1 × 400g bag of kale or spinach

Parmesan cheese (I use a vegetarian one) (optional)

Tomato, miso and sesame soup

This soup comes together in the time it would take for you to nip down the shops for a tin of cream of tomato, but it is much more satisfying and full of goodness. It is a clean, fresh tomato soup – the quick cooking keeps the flavour perky and bright. I add miso and tahini here, which are two of my favourite partners for tomatoes, the earthy creaminess of the tahini and the deep saltiness of the miso backing up the clean tomato flavour like a dream. In the winter, when fresh tomatoes aren't at their best, you could use two 400g tins of tomatoes and forget the fresh ones.

I have suggested a quick topping to take this soup to the next level in flavour terms. If you are really pushed for time, some chopped coriander would suffice.

....

Fill and boil a kettle and get all your ingredients and equipment together. Put a large pan on a low heat.

Working quickly, chop the spring onions and add to the pan with a splash of coconut or olive oil. Turn up the heat to medium and stir from time to time for a couple of minutes until beginning to brown. Chop the fresh tomatoes in half, bigger ones into quarters, and once the spring onions have had a couple of minutes, add them to the pan. Add the tinned tomatoes, fill the can with boiling water and pour this in too, then add the miso paste and bring to the boil.

Meanwhile, make the topping. Mix the honey, tahini, miso and lemon juice in a bowl and put to one side. Toast the sesame seeds in a dry frying pan until golden and chop the coriander.

Once the soup has come to the boil, it's done. Take it off the heat, add the tahini and blitz well with a hand-held blender, adding a little more salt if needed. It should be well balanced between the sweetness of tomatoes, the salty depth of miso and the creamy earthiness of tahini. Ladle into four bowls and top with the miso and honey mix, the sesame seeds and some chopped coriander.

SERVES 4

4 spring onions
coconut or olive oil
500g vine tomatoes
1 × 400g tin of chopped tomatoes
2 tablespoons miso paste
(I use a dark barley miso)
1 tablespoon tahini

FOR THE TOPPING
1 tablespoon runny honey
1 tablespoon tahini
1 tablespoon miso paste
the juice of ½ a lemon
4 tablespoons sesame seeds
a small bunch of fresh coriander

Spiced pea and paneer chapattis

These are super-quick and flavour-packed and what I make when I want some serious flavours but don't have much time. Here, sweet lemon-spiked peas are mashed and piled on to warm chapattis, then topped with crispy cauliflower and heady spices. Finish with a little crispy paneer (I show you how to make it on page 248) if that takes your fancy.

....

Fill and boil a kettle and get all your ingredients and equipment together. Put a griddle pan on a high heat.

Finely slice the spring onions, put into a pan with a little coconut oil and fry on a medium heat until just turning golden. Put the peas into a heatproof mixing bowl, pour boiling water over them and leave for 5 minutes.

Chop the cauliflower into small florets and add to the spring onion pan with the curry leaves and spices. Cook for 2–3 minutes, until the cauliflower has lost its rawness and is coated with the spices, then turn the heat up, squeeze over the juice of 1 lemon and allow to evaporate, then take off the heat.

MAKES 4 FLATBREADS

a small bunch of spring onions

1 tablespoon coconut oil

250g frozen peas

1 small cauliflower

a small handful of curry leaves

2 teaspoons mustard seeds

1 teaspoon ground turmeric

2 unwaxed lemons

1 green chilli

a small bunch of fresh coriander

150g paneer (optional)

4 rotis or chapattis

a small bunch of fresh mint

Chop the green chilli and the stalks of the coriander. Put the leaves aside. Drain and mash the peas with the zest of the other lemon and juice of half, the green chilli and coriander stalks and a good pinch of salt and pepper.

If you are using the paneer, transfer the cauliflower into a bowl and put the pan back on the heat. Add a little coconut oil and once it's really hot, crumble in the paneer; cook on a high heat for a minute or two until the crumbles of cheese crisp up.

Warm the rotis or chapattis in a dry pan or over your gas flame until warm and crisped at the edges. Top with the pea mash, the cauliflower and the crispy paneer, then chop the mint and coriander leaves and scatter over the top.

Soft green herb omelette

This is what I make when reserves are low in every sense of the word, and it's a great way to use up the last bits of a few bunches of herbs.

Omelettes are my ultimate quick dinner and one of my favourite meals – you can put a perfect one on the table in under 15 minutes. For lots more ideas on how to put them together, see pages 34–5. I make my omelettes soft and curdy and just set, and I like them simply spiked with a generous amount of heady soft herbs. Sometimes I skip any filling, as I like the clean simplicity, and I serve mine with a shock of peppery rocket in a punchy vinaigrette.

You can use whatever soft herbs you have to hand – my favourite combination is basil, mint, dill and tarragon. The quality of eggs you use here is absolutely key, there is no hiding, and you want the best you can get your hands on, organic or farm eggs with paint-pot yellow yolks.

SERVES 2

4 free-range or organic eggs

2 small bunches of soft herbs, a mix of any of the following: mint, parsley, dill, chives, tarragon, chervil, basil

a little butter or coconut oil

FILLING

a small handful of goat's, feta or ricotta cheese

a good grating of lemon zest (unwaxed lemon)

a handful of shredded spinach or greens

TO SERVE

a couple of handfuls of rocket or watercress

Get all your ingredients and equipment together. You need a large non-stick frying pan.

Crack your eggs into a bowl, add a healthy pinch of salt and a good bit of freshly ground black pepper and whisk with a fork. Finely chop all the herbs and add them to the eggs.

Heat your frying pan on a medium heat and once it's hot add the butter or oil, allow it to bubble, then lift and tilt the pan so the butter covers the surface.

Put it back on the hob, then, with the fork still nearby, pour the eggs into the pan and allow them to sit untouched for 20 seconds or so, until they begin to set. Now use the fork to pull the omelette away from the edge of the pan into the middle, angling the pan so the egg runs back into the bit you have just exposed. Do this another five or six times in different places

so you have undulating waves of sunshine-yellow egg. Now leave your omelette to cook until it is almost set, which should take a minute or two.

If you are going to fill your omelette, now is the time. Scatter the fillings on one half of the omlette, then flip the other side over to form a half-moon shape and cook for another 30 seconds.

Your omelette should be just set in the middle, still soft and curdy, just turning golden in patches on the outside. Once it's perfect, slide the omelette out of the pan on to a warm plate and serve immediately with a shock of dressed salad.

Too hot salad

I make this when it feels too hot to eat or I am in need of something a bit refreshing. I first made it on a weighty, humid summer's day in London, one of those hot city days when the air doesn't move and all you can think about is swimming pools and ice lollies. Now every time I make this I start singing Kool and the Gang.

The key here is to get everything nice and cold. Search out raw red-skinned peanuts if you can. In the summer I soak a few handfuls in cold water overnight and keep them cool in the fridge for snacking. They are also great in stir-fries and on top of morning fruit. They are fresh and juicy and completely different to a roasted peanut. You can easily find them in health food stores or Indian supermarkets.

For a heartier meal, serve this with cooked and cooled brown basmati rice or some thin rice vermicelli noodles.

....

SERVES 4

50g raw peanuts
(see note in introduction)

2 carrots

200g watermelon

a handful of cherry tomatoes

1 cucumber

1 little gem or 1 cos lettuce,
or ½ an iceberg

a bunch of fresh coriander

FOR THE DRESSING

½ a red chilli

1 tablespoon soy sauce or tamari

2 limes

a little runny honey

Get all your ingredients and equipment together. Soak the peanuts in iced water and put them into the fridge while you get on with everything else.

Peel the carrots, then use a speed-peeler to peel them into long strips and place them in a bowl with some iced water.

Cut the watermelon into bite-size pieces, removing any very seedy bits and the outer skin. Halve the cherry tomatoes. Pop both into a serving bowl and put into the fridge.

Use the speed-peeler to peel the cucumber into long strips too, stopping when you get to the watery seeded bit, and add to the serving bowl of watermelon and tomatoes in the fridge. Shred the lettuce and pick the coriander leaves from the stalks.

Too hot salad

Chop the red chilli for the dressing and put into a small bowl with the soy, the juice of both limes and a small squeeze of honey. Taste and adjust, adding more lime, honey and soy if needed until you have a nice balance of heat, acidity and sweetness.

Take the serving bowl and the peanuts out of the fridge. Drain the peanuts and carrots well, add to the bowl and pour over the dressing. Toss through the lettuce and scatter over the coriander. Eat in a breezy spot, while thinking of dipping your feet in the pool.

10 favourite omelette fillings

An omelette is one of the ultimate quick dinners. These are my 10 favourite omelette fillings, but follow this pattern and you can't go wrong: main veg – back-up veg – accent flavour – back-up flavour – richness.

See page 28 for my favourite way to make an omelette, and remember to buy the best eggs you can.

	MAIN VEG →	**BACK-UP VEG** →
1	Sauté 100g of spinach	With 50g of halved cherry tomatoes
2	Slice and fry a red onion until soft	Add a handful of shredded greens
3	Fry some sliced leftover potatoes	With a few roasted red peppers from a jar
4	Sauté 100g of greens	Add ½ a mashed avocado
5	Sauté a handful of mushrooms	With a handful of spinach
6	Finely slice and sauté some asparagus	With 1 finely sliced courgette
7	Sauté some grated squash	With a handful of cooked chickpeas
8	Cook a handful of peas	With a handful of broad beans
9	Sauté a grated carrot	With a handful of chopped mint
10	Fry 1 small leek until soft	Add a handful of mushrooms

ACCENT FLAVOUR →	BACK-UP FLAVOUR →	RICHNESS
Add a few basil leaves	25g of toasted pine nuts	Finish with a good grating of pecorino
Add the leaves from 2 sprigs of thyme	Add a splash of balsamic vinegar	Add a crumbling of goat's cheese
Add a handful of chopped parsley	A good pinch of smoked paprika	Add a grating of Manchego
Tear in a few basil leaves	Add the zest and juice of ½ a lemon	Finish with a crumbling of feta
Add ½ a chopped chilli	And the juice of a lemon	Finish with a grating of Parmesan
Mix in a tablespoon of pesto	Grate in the zest of ½ a lemon	And a little crumble of goat's cheese
Add a teaspoon of harissa	Grate in the zest of a lemon	Add a final crumbling of feta
Add a small handful of chopped mint	Squeeze in the juice of ½ a lemon	Add a good drizzle of olive oil
Stir in some toasted almonds	Squeeze in the juice of ½ a lemon	Top with a crumbling of feta or paneer
Add the leaves from a few sprigs of tarragon or dill	Add a teaspoon of mustard	Add a small handful of grated Cheddar

Gently spiced sweet potato and quinoa bowls

The first time we made this was one of those moments where a few things pulled out of the fridge were thrown together for a quick dinner and the stars aligned to make something brilliant. It is, in fact, John's recipe. He is amazing at cooking quick nutritious food, and about the only person I know who really truly honestly in his heart of hearts would prefer a bowl of vegetables to just about anything else.

You can have this on your table in about 15 minutes and it uses quinoa in a way I would never have considered, yet it is so good. Here, coconut and turmeric are backed up by minerally greens and a final shock of lemon. Good, quick, tasty eating.

I use chard, but spring greens or even spinach would work just fine. Creamed coconut instead of coconut milk gives a more intense flavour and lends itself well to quick cooking.

SERVES 3

150g quinoa

1 teaspoon vegetable stock powder, or ½ a stock cube

4 spring onions

1 clove of garlic

coconut oil

2 teaspoons mustard seeds (I use black)

2 carrots

1 sweet potato

½ × 200g pack of creamed coconut

1 teaspoon ground turmeric

½ × 400g tin of chickpeas, or 250g home-cooked chickpeas (see pages 241–5)

400g bunch of chard or spring greens

1 lemon

Fill and boil a kettle and get all your ingredients and equipment together.

Weigh out the quinoa in a mug or measuring jug, making note of the level it comes up to, quickly rinse it under cold water, then pour it into a large saucepan. Fill the mug to the same level with boiling water and add to the pan, then repeat so you have double the volume of water to quinoa. Add the stock powder or cube, then put the pan on a high heat, put the lid on and cook the quinoa at a steady simmer for 10–12 minutes, until almost all the water has been absorbed and the little curly grain has been released from each quinoa seed.

Meanwhile, chop the spring onions into thin rounds. Peel and finely slice the garlic. Put a saucepan on a medium heat and add a knob of coconut oil. Throw in the spring onions and cook for a couple of minutes, then add the garlic and the mustard seeds and cook until the seeds begin to pop.

Peel the carrots and cut in half lengthways and then into thin slices, then do the same with the sweet potato. It's important that the slices are thin, so that the vegetables cook quickly. Add them to the pan and cook for a minute before adding the creamed coconut, turmeric, drained chickpeas, 400ml of hot water and a good pinch of salt. Bring to the boil and simmer for 5 minutes, until the sweet potato is soft.

Keep an eye on your quinoa – it should have absorbed all the water by now, and the little curly grain should be visible. If it is, turn off the heat and leave the lid on.

Finally, cut the leaves off the chard or greens and shred them finely, then finely slice the stalks. Heat a tiny bit of coconut oil in a frying pan, add the stalks and fry for a minute, then add the leaves and sauté until wilted – this will take 2–3 minutes.

Once the sweet potato is cooked, stir the quinoa into the coconut and sweet potato. Serve in deep bowls, with the chard on top, and finish with a squeeze of lemon.

Smoky pepper and white bean quesadillas

Quesadillas, like a lot of Mexican food, get a bad write-up as being cheese-laden and lazy, but they are a truly quick meal, and by filling them with not just cheese they become more nourishing and much more delicious.

Here I have stepped away from the straight-up Mexican quesadillas and introduced some Spanish flavours. Roasted red peppers, smoky paprika and white beans – it makes me think of summer trips to Barcelona, and that can never be a bad thing.

If you are vegan, leave the cheese out and double the white beans, which hold it all together; you may want to be more generous with the seasoning too. I mostly make these at lunchtime, but they are filling enough for a dinner – you might want some sherry-vinegar-dressed green salad on the side.

If you are making these for a party, which I often do, the filling can be made in bigger batches really easily. The quesadillas can be stacked in the fridge, filled, and ready for frying.

....

Get all your ingredients together.

Finely slice the spring onions. Put a frying pan on a medium heat, add a little olive oil, the spring onions and smoked paprika, and cook for a couple of minutes, until starting to brown.

Meanwhile, put the white beans into a mixing bowl and mash them with a fork, then roughly chop your red peppers and add half of them to the beans. Grate over the zest of the lemon, then roughly chop the parsley and add half to the bowl. Grate in your Manchego. Once the spring onions are browned, add these too.

Lay a tortilla or wrap on your work surface. Spoon the red pepper mixture all over it, spread it evenly, then top with the other tortilla. Heat a frying

SERVES 2 (MAKES 1 DEEPLY FILLED QUESADILLA)

2 spring onions
olive oil
½ teaspoon smoked paprika
50g cooked white beans
100g jarred, roasted red peppers
1 unwaxed lemon
½ a bunch of fresh parsley
50g Manchego cheese
(see note for vegans)
2 wholemeal or seeded tortillas
or wraps
a handful of cherry tomatoes

pan and toast the quesadilla for a couple of minutes on each side –
I do this dry, but you can add a splash of oil if you like your quesadillas
crispy. If you find it hard to flip, a plate on top might help.

While the quesadilla is toasting, roughly chop the tomatoes, mix with the
remaining peppers and parsley and squeeze in the juice of half the lemon.

Once toasted on both sides, remove the quesadilla from the pan and cut into
six pieces. Serve in the middle of the table, with the salsa for spooning over.

Green pea and coconut soup

When I am hungry and impatient and I have nothing in the fridge this simple soup is the recipe I turn to.

For a really speedy soup the pan you use is important; a small deep saucepan will mean your soup won't come to a simmer quickly, so I suggest a deep, wide saucepan. Cast iron is ideal as it conducts the heat evenly, so even though you are cooking quickly it's less likely that your soup will catch on the bottom. Of course use what you have, but a good deep heavy-bottomed saucepan is a great investment.

If you don't have spring onions, a normal onion will do fine – you may just need to cook it for a little longer.

....

Fill and boil a kettle and get all your ingredients and equipment together. Put a large soup pan, one that has a lid, on a medium heat to warm up.

Chop the spring onions quite finely and put into the pan with the coconut oil. Turn up the heat to its highest and cook for 2 minutes, until softened.

Add the peas to the pan with the coconut milk, the stock powder or cube and 750ml of boiling water, then put a lid on and bring to the boil. Once boiling, simmer, still on a high heat, for 2–3 minutes.

Take off the heat. Add most of the herbs, stalks and all, and the juice of the lemon and use a stick blender to blitz the soup until super-smooth.

Serve ladled into bowls with a little olive oil and the rest of the green herbs.

SERVES 4–6

a bunch of spring onions
1 teaspoon coconut oil
1kg frozen peas
1 × 400ml tin of coconut milk
1 tablespoon vegetable stock powder, or ½ a stock cube
a bunch of basil or coriander (or a mixture of both)
1 lemon

TO SERVE
extra virgin olive oil

Pour-over soup

This soup is the epitome of quick cooking. Finely sliced vegetables, delicate noodles and flavour-packed aromatics all come together to make a soup that's ready in the time it takes to boil the kettle. Most of the cooking is done by adding the boiling water from the kettle, so no pans, just a couple of bowls and a bit of chopping.

You can mix and match the veg you use here for variety, but just make sure they are ones that will be edible with very little cooking – greens, finely sliced carrots, grated squash, sliced mushrooms all work well.

This is a great, healthy meal to take to work if that's your thing; just keep it in the fridge and pour over the hot water at your desk.

....

Fill and boil the kettle and get all your ingredients out. You'll need two heatproof mixing bowls with a plate that fits on top.

Once the kettle has boiled, put the noodles into one of the mixing bowls and cover with boiling water. Leave to sit, covered with a plate.

Peel the ginger and grate into the other bowl, then add the creamed coconut, white miso, sesame oil, soy or tamari and star anise. Very finely slice the spring onion and the chilli and add most of them to the bowl. Shred the greens, cut the courgette into thin slices and slice the sugar snaps. Add them all to the bowl.

Once the noodles have had 3 minutes, drain them and add them to the bowl of green veg. If you're making for lunch later, layer everything into a screwtop jar and finish the recipe when you're ready to eat. Re-boil the kettle. Pour over hot water from the kettle until the noodles and veg are just covered, and mix well.

Garnish with the remaining chopped chilli and spring onion, a little basil or coriander and some toasted sesame seeds.

SERVES 1

50g thin rice vermicelli
(I use brown rice ones)
a small piece of fresh ginger
1 tablespoon creamed coconut
a good spoonful of white miso paste
a splash of sesame oil
1 tablespoon soy sauce or tamari
1 star anise
1 spring onion
1 fresh red chilli
a small handful of greens
½ a courgette
a small handful of sugar snap peas

TO SERVE

a few sprigs of fresh basil
or coriander
1 tablespoon toasted sesame seeds

at your desk salads

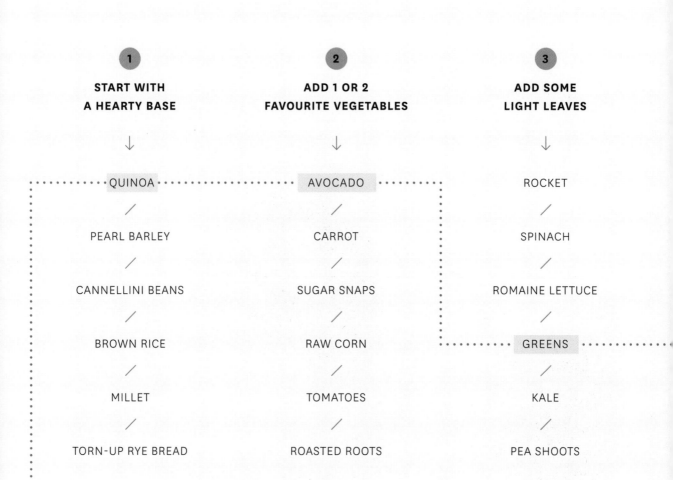

1	**2**	**3**
START WITH A HEARTY BASE	**ADD 1 OR 2 FAVOURITE VEGETABLES**	**ADD SOME LIGHT LEAVES**
↓	↓	↓
QUINOA	AVOCADO	ROCKET
PEARL BARLEY	CARROT	SPINACH
CANNELLINI BEANS	SUGAR SNAPS	ROMAINE LETTUCE
BROWN RICE	RAW CORN	GREENS
MILLET	TOMATOES	KALE
TORN-UP RYE BREAD	ROASTED ROOTS	PEA SHOOTS

EXAMPLE

Lunch on the run or at your desk can be dull and samey. Use this guide to make your own quick salads. Using a grain or pulse as a base will mean it is filling, and its hardiness means your salad will travel well.

Take one element from each column and stack in a wide jar or Tupperware, making sure you work in layers from the heaviest (grains) to the lightest (leaves).

Make a dressing in a small jam jar, or pour it into a small bowl lined with clingfilm, bring the ends together and twist to make a little dressing wrap. I mix one of the suggested dressing flavours with 1 tablespoon of olive oil and a good squeeze of lemon juice, salt and pepper. The nutrition from salad leaves is actually boosted when we dress them, as the good fat from the oil makes it easier for our bodies to take up the nutrients.

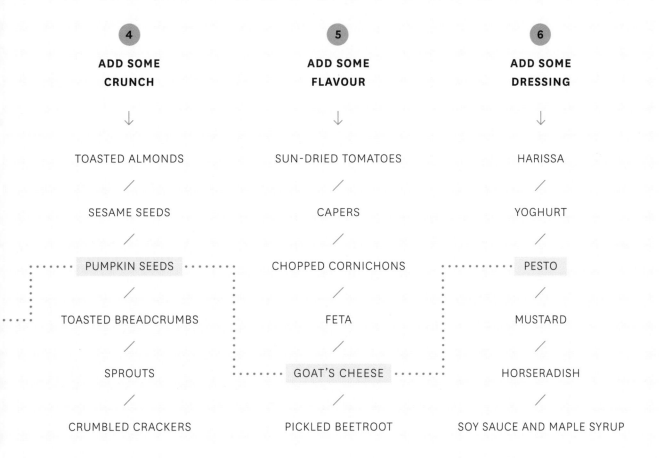

4

**ADD SOME
CRUNCH**

↓

TOASTED ALMONDS

/

SESAME SEEDS

/

PUMPKIN SEEDS

/

TOASTED BREADCRUMBS

/

SPROUTS

/

CRUMBLED CRACKERS

5

**ADD SOME
FLAVOUR**

↓

SUN-DRIED TOMATOES

/

CAPERS

/

CHOPPED CORNICHONS

/

FETA

/

GOAT'S CHEESE

/

PICKLED BEETROOT

6

**ADD SOME
DRESSING**

↓

HARISSA

/

YOGHURT

/

PESTO

/

MUSTARD

/

HORSERADISH

/

SOY SAUCE AND MAPLE SYRUP

Two favourite sandwiches

Sandwiches are unbeatable. They are super-quick, usually pretty cheap, and as long as you get yourself some good bread and stuff them with a bit of veg they can be super-good for you too.

Everyone has their favourite sandwich; these are the two that are made most in my kitchen. Both require 5 minutes' work but you'll be glad you took the extra time. These recipes have been written for one sandwich but can easily be scaled up for more. They both work really well on rye bread too.

KALE SMASH, HONEYED CARROT AND HUMMUS

MAKES 1 SANDWICH

a handful of kale
2 sun-dried tomatoes
1 lemon
extra virgin olive oil
1 small carrot
a little squeeze of honey
2 slices of good sourdough bread
1 tablespoon hummus
a handful of lettuce leaves, shredded
(I use Little Gem)

Get all your ingredients together.

Put the kale into a food processor with the sun-dried tomatoes, a squeeze of lemon juice, a tablespoon of olive oil and a pinch of salt and pepper. Blitz until you have a paste.

Next, peel and finely slice the carrot, put it into a pan with the honey, a little olive oil, salt and pepper, and cook until just softened and not too crunchy.

Toast your bread, then spread one slice thickly with the kale smash and one with hummus. Put the carrots on top of the hummus, add a little shredded lettuce and sandwich together.

MAKES 1 SANDWICH
(AND A SMALL JAR OF PESTO)

2 slices of multi-grain
or sourdough bread

50g pecorino cheese (vegetarian)

1 teaspoon thick honey

extra virgin olive oil

FOR THE QUICK SAGE PESTO

100g raw almonds
(preferably soaked)

zest of 1 unwaxed lemon and
½ the juice

2 sprigs of sage leaves

a pinch of sea salt

2 tablespoons extra virgin olive oil

SAGE AND LEMON PESTO, PECORINO AND HONEY

Get all your ingredients together.

First make your sage pesto. Blitz all the ingredients until you have a chunky pesto, and season with more salt and pepper to taste.

Heat a frying pan on a medium heat. Slather one slice of bread thickly with the sage pesto, then slice the pecorino thinly and lay it on top. Spread the honey on the other slice and sandwich together. Drizzle the outsides of the sandwich with a little olive oil then put into the pan and toast on both sides until golden, using a spatula to press down as needed.

Once the sandwich is toasted and golden, cut in half and devour.

Avocado, tahini and olive smash flatbreads

I try to sneak avocados in anywhere I can. I love their buttery, grassy, rich creaminess. The last five years has seen avocado on toast elbow its way on to every breakfast and lunch menu in the land. Avocado on toast was something I grew up on, and my love of avos has undoubtedly been inherited from my mum.

So I thought it was time to mix things up a bit, still making the most of how instantly delicious an avocado is but adding some more unusual flavours. Here I smash avocados with tahini, olives and lemon to make one of my new favourite lunches.

This is equally good on toast. I often double the recipe and serve it in bowls with home-made tortilla chips, to make an amazing snack for a crowd.

....

Get all your ingredients together.

Halve and de-stone the avocados and scoop the flesh into a bowl with a good pinch of salt and pepper. Squeeze over the juice of the lemon and the clementine or orange. Add the tahini and roughly smash and mash until you have a half smooth, half chunky mixture.

De-stone and roughly chop the olives and add them to the bowl. Very finely chop or grate the garlic and add that to the bowl too. Gently mix to combine.

Heat the flatbreads either in a dry frying pan or on an open gas flame, turning them with tongs once they have browned a little. This will take a few seconds on a gas hob and more like 30 seconds to 1 minute in a pan.

Cut the flatbreads into quarters and pile on the avocado mixture. Top with a scattering of chilli flakes, toasted cumin seeds and a few delicate herbs. If you like you can add a crumble of feta.

SERVES 2 AS A LUNCH,
OR 4 AS A SNACK

2 ripe avocados
½ a lemon
1 clementine, or ½ an orange
2 tablespoons tahini
2 handfuls of Kalamata olives
½ a small clove of garlic

TO SERVE
4 flatbreads or tortillas
chilli flakes
toasted cumin seeds
fresh green herbs
(I use dill, basil or parsley)
feta cheese (optional)

Avocado, cucumber and fennel soup

This soup couldn't be easier and is one of the quickest recipes I've ever made. It's what I eat on hot days or days when I feel like something light, refreshing and cleansing. I don't think that this kind of super-fresh food should be banished from the winter though. I have been known to eat a bowl of this in front of the fire in January after the Christmas eating enthusiasm.

I mention using avocado oil here; if you don't have it, a good extra virgin olive oil will be great, but avocado oil has such an amazing buttery taste that it is worth searching out. Use it anywhere you might use good olive oil, to finish soups and in dressings.

SERVES 2 AS A MEAL,
OR 4 AS A STARTER

1 ripe avocado

1 cucumber

½ a large bulb of fennel

2 tablespoons Greek
or coconut yoghurt

the juice of ½ a lemon

a handful of ice cubes

a few sprigs of fresh dill

a few sprigs of fresh basil

½ a green chilli

a handful of toasted
pumpkin seeds

extra virgin olive oil
or avocado oil

Get all your ingredients together.

De-stone the avocado and scoop the flesh into the jug of a blender. Chop the cucumber and fennel into large pieces and add these too, along with the yoghurt, lemon juice, ice cubes and a good pinch of salt and pepper. Blitz on high until you have a completely smooth pale green soup. Taste the soup and add more lemon or salt if needed; the flavour should be subtle and refreshing, with a back-note of lemon.

Once the soup is completely smooth, pour into bowls and top with fronds of dill, little basil leaves, chopped green chilli, some pumpkin seeds and a good drizzle of oil. If it's a really hot day you can add a couple more ice cubes too.

ready
in twenty

Life-friendly dinners, layered with a rainbow of veg, for when you have a dash more time. These are hearty dinners: generous salads, hash browns and home-made beans, quick-as-a-flash Vietnamese noodles, rainbow goodness bowls, quick stews, vibrant nachos, roasted lemon courgetti and quick quinoa risotto.

Early summer greens goddess salad

Coconuts and avocados are two of my favourite things and luckily they are a happy pairing. Here they join forces to create an incredible dinner salad as fresh and zippy as it is satisfying. This dressing is inspired by the famous Green Goddess dressing I loved so much growing up in San Francisco. My version has some coconut milk and a kick from rice wine vinegar and soy.

Search out the ripest avocados, as this salad is really a love song to their creamy grassy deliciousness. When asparagus isn't around I make this with purple sprouting broccoli. If I am really hungry I add some cooked and cooled buckwheat noodles, quinoa or brown rice to my bowl too.

....

Fill and boil a kettle and get all your ingredients and equipment together.

Put a frying pan on a high heat. Chop the asparagus stalks into 1cm coins, leaving the tips intact. Add a little oil to the pan and add all the asparagus. Cook for a couple of minutes to take off the raw edge, then take the pan off the heat.

Place the sugar snaps in a bowl (I like to cut them in half down the middle, but you can leave them whole to save time) with the edamame beans. Cover with boiling water and leave to one side.

Now make the dressing. Scoop half an avocado into a blender (or use a deep bowl and a stick blender). Add the coconut milk, honey, chilli, half the basil and coriander (stalks and all), the soy and vinegar and blitz until smooth and green. Taste, and add more soy, vinegar or honey, if needed.

Put the spinach into a serving bowl. Drain the sugar snaps and edamame well and add them to the spinach with the asparagus. Cut the avocado in half and take out the stone, then use a knife to criss-cross both halves all the way to the skin. Using a spoon, scoop the avocado flesh into the bowl. Finish by topping with the dressing, the rest of the basil and coriander leaves and the sesame seeds.

SERVES 4

a bunch of asparagus
olive oil
400g sugar snap peas
300g edamame beans
300g baby spinach
1 ripe avocado
50g toasted white or black sesame seeds

FOR THE DRESSING
½ a ripe avocado
4 tablespoons coconut milk
a squeeze of runny honey or agave syrup
1 green chilli
a small bunch of fresh basil
a small bunch of fresh coriander
2 tablespoons tamari or light soy sauce
4 tablespoons rice wine vinegar

Butter beans with fennel, lemon and tomato

I buy Greek gigantes beans – tomato-and-dill-spiked buttery beans generously coated in olive oil – in jars from my local shop and feast on them with flatbreads when I'm feeling lazy. This is how I make them at home, more of a quick stew, with heady lemon, caramelised fennel and some fennel seeds, which is my nod to the traditional shot of ouzo. I haven't added as much oil as the Greeks often do, but if you like things richer you can add a generous drizzle at the end. I often serve this with feta, warm flatbreads and some leaves.

SERVES 4

1 large bulb of fennel

olive oil

a small bunch of spring onions

2 cloves of garlic

200g cherry tomatoes

1 lemon

½ teaspoon fennel seeds

1 tablespoon dried oregano, or a small handful of chopped fresh oregano

a pinch of dried chilli flakes

1 tablespoon runny honey

1 tablespoon red wine vinegar

2 × 400g tins of cooked white beans, or 250g home-cooked beans (see pages 241–5)

a small bunch of fresh dill

First prepare the fennel. Remove the bulb's tough outside layer, then trim and slice along the length of the bulb through the root into 1cm slices.

Heat a large heavy frying pan over a medium-high heat and add a good drizzle of olive oil. When the pan is hot and the oil starts to ripple, add the fennel, spreading it out so one flat side hits the pan. Cook for about 2 minutes, until browned and caramelised, then turn over and cook for another 2 minutes. Meanwhile, chop the spring onions and garlic. Once the fennel is browned, add the spring onions and garlic to the pan and stir for a couple of minutes.

Chop the tomatoes and cut the lemon into wedges, then add both to the pan with the fennel seeds, oregano, chilli flakes, honey and vinegar. Let the liquid heat and reduce for a minute or so before adding the beans and 100ml of water. Cook until the beans are warmed through – about 5 minutes.

Chop the dill and scatter over to finish, along with a drizzle of good olive oil.

20 MINUTES

Smoky beans and sweet potato hash browns

Nothing fancy here. Just a good quick dinner, which doubles as a favourite brunch too. If you like, add a fried egg to top it off.

If you are vegan or don't eat eggs, you can use 2 tablespoons of chia seeds mixed with 6 tablespoons of water to bind the hash browns instead of the eggs.

....

Finely chop the shallot or onion, put it into a hot pan with a little oil, and cook for 4–5 minutes, until browned.

Meanwhile grate your sweet potatoes into a big mixing bowl, add a good pinch of salt and pepper, the cumin seeds and the eggs, and mix together well.

When the onions are beginning to brown, add the smoked paprika and cook for a minute. Roughly chop the tomatoes and add to the pan, then drain the beans and add these too, along with a splash of balsamic and the leaves from the thyme. Add a good pinch of salt and pepper and cook for 5 minutes, until the sauce has thickened and the tomatoes have broken down.

Heat a little oil in a large frying pan. Divide the sweet potato mixture roughly into 4 and use your hands to make a rough patty, then carefully put into the pan to fry. Do this with the rest of the mix, so you have 4 patties. Cook on a low to medium heat for 4–6 minutes, until golden brown, then use a fish slice to carefully flip and cook for another 4–6 minutes. As they cook, use the fish slice to gently push down on them to pack everything together.

Serve the hash with the beans and, if you like, a fried egg or some dressed leaves.

SERVES 2

1 shallot or ½ a red onion
a little olive oil
2 sweet potatoes (about 500g)
½ teaspoon cumin seeds
2 free-range or organic eggs
½ teaspoon smoked paprika
100g cherry tomatoes
1 × 400g tin of cannellini beans
a dash of balsamic vinegar
a few sprigs of fresh thyme

Kale, sumac and crispy rice salad

This is an amazing salad based on one I ate at an incredible neighbourhood café in LA. Sqirl is one of those places where you want every single thing on the menu, right down to the drinks. On my last trip to LA I ate there five times. For someone who doesn't like routine that's pretty solid. This is a play on what was my favourite thing on the menu. It has inspired flavours with sumac and lime, and textures with kale and crispy rice.

I am going to ask you to cook your rice three times here, which may seem crazy, but it'll create perfect little pops of crunch against the rest of the salad. This is a great way to use up leftover rice too – just skip the first cooking stage. It's also really good topped with a softly poached egg or some feta and flatbreads if you are hungry.

Bear in mind that if you use brown rice it will take about 20 minutes to cook.

....

Fill and boil a kettle and get all your ingredients and a large frying pan together.

Cook the rice in a small saucepan of boiling salted water until cooked – this will take 10–15 minutes.

Meanwhile, pull the kale from its stems and shred the leaves with a knife or tear into small pieces with your hands. Put the leaves into a bowl, then add the zest and juice of the lemon and a good pinch of salt and scrunch it in your hands for a minute to break it down a little. Chop the spring onions finely and add them to the bowl.

Once the rice is cooked, drain it well. Put a large frying pan on the heat and when it's hot, add the rice with no oil and dry-fry for a couple of minutes to get rid of any moisture.

Remove the rice from the pan, then put the pan back on the heat, add half the coconut oil at a time and fry the rice in two batches until starting to

SERVES 4 AS A LIGHT MEAL,
2 AS A MAIN

100g basmati rice (I use brown)

a bunch of curly kale, green or purple (about 200g)

the zest and juice of 1 unwaxed lemon

3 spring onions

2 tablespoons coconut oil

the zest and juice of 1 unwaxed lime

1 tablespoon sumac (optional)

2 tablespoons good olive oil

1 teaspoon runny honey

6 medjool dates

turn lightly brown and really crispy. Drain on kitchen paper and sprinkle with salt.

Now make your dressing. Put the zest and juice of the lime into a screwtop jar with the sumac, if using, and 2 tablespoons of olive oil, add the honey and a pinch of salt and pepper. Put on the lid and shake to combine.

De-stone and roughly chop the dates and add to the kale. Once the rice is almost cool, add it to the kale and toss in the dressing.

20 MINUTES

Lemongrass, peanut and herb bun cha

SERVES 2

FOR THE TOFU

200g firm tofu

1 red chilli

1 clove of garlic

½ a stalk of fresh lemongrass

1 tablespoon soy sauce or tamari

1 lime

1 tablespoon peanut butter

coconut oil

FOR THE NOODLES AND VEG

125g rice vermicelli

½ a small iceberg lettuce

1 large carrot

½ a cucumber

2 spring onions

½ a ripe avocado

a small bunch of fresh coriander

50g unsalted peanuts

a small bunch of fresh mint
or other herbs (see introduction)

FOR THE DRESSING

2 teaspoons runny honey
or maple syrup

1 tablespoon soy sauce or tamari

the juice of 2 limes

You can't live in east London and fail to be inspired by the endless and sometimes brilliant Vietnamese restaurants that line the streets of Hackney. Outside London, though, it's harder to lay your hands on the bright fresh food I love so much.

This bun cha is a fragrant, delicate rice noodle salad. I have taken the original Hanoi recipe and made my own chilli-spiked tofu version, half noodles, half salad, all flavour. I eat this when it's hot or when I need something clean and cleansing. Here many of my favourite things jump into the same bowl: crispy tofu, bright and zippy vegetables, grassy avocado and sprightly herbs.

If you can get your hands on them, some Vietnamese herbs would take this bun cha to the next level – Vietnamese basil, mint, coriander and pasilla – but I've kept it simple with some mint and coriander here.

First, chop the tofu into 0.5cm fingers and put into a bowl. Finely chop the chilli and finely chop the garlic and the lemongrass stalk, then put half the chilli and garlic aside for later and add the rest to the bowl of tofu with all the lemongrass, the soy sauce and the juice of half the lime. Put the tofu to one side.

Mix the juice from the other lime half with the peanut butter and a splash of water and put to one side.

Next, put the noodles into a bowl, cover with boiling water and leave to soak for 3 minutes, or follow the packet instructions.

Now chop the vegetables – you can use a food processor or a mandolin to speed this up. Shred the iceberg and cut the carrot and cucumber into matchsticks. Finely slice the spring onions and slice the avocado thinly. Roughly chop the coriander and then the peanuts.

Make the dressing by mixing the reserved chilli and garlic with the rest of the dressing ingredients.

Heat a pan and add a little coconut oil. Drain the tofu, reserving the marinade. Once the pan is hot, add the tofu to the pan and fry until browned on all sides, then add the peanut butter mixture and the reserved marinade and toss to coat. Take off the heat.

Pile the drained noodles into two bowls and top with the vegetables, coriander, peanuts and the mint or herb sprigs. Finally, put the tofu and any of the marinade left in the pan on top and pour over the dressing. Mix up at the table.

goodness bowls

I make a goodness bowl for myself at least once a week; they are a quick, easy and totally adaptable dinner which can be tweaked throughout the seasons to be hearty, light, refreshing – whatever you feel like. I have laid out the building blocks and given you some examples of my favourites. Check out my recipes for Seeded halloumi and harissa rainbow bowl (page 76) and Plantain, avocado and black bean bowl (page 68) to get the idea.

Here are some of the ingredients I use most often. Pick from each column. Make a dressing with 1 part acid (lemon/vinegar) to 2 parts oil and you can't go wrong.

HEARTINESS: GRAIN/PULSE	→	2–4 SEASONAL VEG	→
quinoa		shaved raw beets	
millet		scrunched greens	
amaranth		sautéed carrots	
pulses		roasted butternut	
pearl barley		roasted sweet potato	
soba noodles		sautéed potato	
		pan-fried mushrooms	
		grated carrot	
		roast celeriac	
		tomatoes	
		roast cauliflower	
		steamed broccoli	
		blanched kale	
		avocado	

SOME FAVOURITE COMBINATIONS

1	quinoa	→	kale peas broccoli	→	
2	brown rice	→	spinach carrots sugar snaps	→	
3	butter beans	→	greens sweet potatoes tomatoes	→	

A FLAVOUR BOOSTER →	A KILLER DRESSING →	HERBS →	FINISHING TOUCH/ TEXTURE
sautéed onions	miso	parsley	toasted nuts
sautéed leeks	harissa	coriander	toasted seeds
roasted jarred red peppers	tahini	fried sage	croutons
sautéed spring onions	mustard	mint	feta
sautéed ginger and garlic	citrus	dill	goat's cheese
pickled red cabbage	pesto	fried thyme	Manchego
sauerkraut	hummus	fried rosemary	Parmesan
	yoghurt	basil	crumbled crackers
	tzatziki	rocket	
	mango chutney		

· ·

	→		→		→	
sautéed spring onions		harissa lemon extra virgin olive oil		mint parsley		toasted almonds
crispy fried onions		sesame oil soy sauce rice wine vinegar		coriander		toasted sesame seeds
roasted red peppers		lemon olive oil smoked paprika		parsley		toasted sourdough, crumbled

Plantain, avocado
and black bean bowl

Sometimes I fall head over heels for a food and I can't stop eating it. For a few weeks this year it was plantain. It fills the greengrocers around where I live and I almost always pass my hand over it to reach for sweet potatoes or parsnips. Well, no more. Plantain is my new sweet potato; it adds natural sweetness to my dinners and is super quick to cook and prepare. This dish is my love letter to plantain. I promise I'll never overlook you again.

This bowl is a meeting place for a whole world of flavours: chilli-spiked smoky black beans, caramel-crusted plantain, creamy avo and sweet leeks and zingy lime. It's a serious flavour-filled bowl of goodness.

It also works really well with short-grain brown rice in place of the quinoa. I opt for brown rice when I feel like something more filling, but it takes much longer to cook, so bear that in mind.

....

Fill and boil a kettle and get all your ingredients and equipment together.

Weigh out the quinoa in a mug or measuring jug, making note of the level it comes up to, then pour it into a large saucepan. Fill the mug to the same level with boiling water and add to the pan, then repeat so you have double the volume of water to quinoa. Add the stock powder or cube, put the pan on a high heat and cook the quinoa at a steady simmer for 10–12 minutes, until almost all the water has been absorbed and the little curly grain has been released from each quinoa seed.

Chop the chilli. Pour the black beans (including the liquid) into a pan, add half the chopped chilli and a pinch of cinnamon, and simmer until the beans are thick and almost all the liquid is gone.

Meanwhile, place a pan on a high heat. Trim, wash and finely shred both leeks, add them to the pan with a little coconut oil, sweat for 10 minutes until soft, then tip into a bowl. Chop the mushrooms into bite-size pieces.

SERVES 4

a mugful of quinoa (about 200g)

1 tablespoon of vegetable stock powder, or ½ a stock cube

1 green chilli

1 × 400g tin of black beans

a pinch of ground cinnamon

2 large leeks

coconut oil

2 handfuls of interesting mushrooms (about 250g)

2 ripe avocados

2 limes

2 large plantains

Once the leeks are done, remove them from the pan with a slotted spoon. Put the pan back on the heat and add a little more coconut oil and the mushrooms. Pan-fry until crisp, then add to the bowl of leeks.

Mash the avocados with the other half of the chopped chilli and the juice of one of the limes.

Put the pan back on the heat. Peel the plantains, cut into 1cm-thick slices and add to the pan, allowing each piece to caramelise before turning it over and doing the same on the other side.

Drain the quinoa and divide between four big bowls. Top with the leeks and mushrooms, a few spoonfuls of black beans, and the plantain and finish with a healthy spoonful of mashed chilli avocado and the other lime cut into wedges.

Sweet potato, lime and peanut soup

I started making this soup one January when Christmas had been and gone and I was a little jaded by wintry food. I wanted something warming, filling, refreshing and restoring all at once. It has become the soup that I just can't stop making. It may not sound much, but the beauty of it is in the few ingredients and the simple, zippy but hearty flavour.

The soup is good on its own but, to really make it sing, I spend the time while it's cooking making a crispy topping which I toss with lime zest and some peanuts to amp up the flavour.

The clever bit here is using peanut butter to make the soup delicious and creamy. It's a good hit of protein and adds a deep earthiness. It's important to buy a good one, with no added ingredients like palm oil. I make my own, and store it in pots which last me a month – it's much fresher and I am sure more nourishing, an investment which I use for breakfast and in sauces and soups. (For my nut butter recipes, see page 226.)

SERVES 4

FOR THE SOUP
2 leeks
coconut oil
1kg sweet potatoes (about 4)
a thumb-size piece of fresh ginger
1 tablespoon vegetable stock powder, or ½ a stock cube
1 tablespoon soy sauce or tamari
1 tablespoon maple syrup
1 tablespoon peanut butter

FOR THE TOPPING
1 shallot
a thumb-size piece of fresh ginger
coconut oil
a handful of roasted, unsalted peanuts
2 unwaxed limes

Fill and boil a kettle and get all your ingredients and equipment together. Put a large pan on a low heat.

Trim and wash the leeks and finely shred them. Add a knob of coconut oil to the pan and, once melted, throw in the leeks. Cook on a high heat for 3–4 minutes, stirring from time to time until soft.

While the leeks are cooking, peel the sweet potatoes and chop into rough 1cm dice. Peel and grate the ginger. Once the leeks are cooked, add the sweet potatoes and ginger with 1.5 litres of hot water from the kettle and the stock powder or cube, then bring to the boil and simmer for 10 minutes, until the potatoes are cooked. Top up with more hot water if needed.

Meanwhile, for the topping, put a frying pan on a high heat. Peel and finely slice the shallot and grate the second piece of ginger. Put a knob of coconut

oil into the hot pan, then add the shallot and ginger and fry until really crisp. Drain on kitchen paper. Roughly chop the peanuts and put them into a bowl. Grate over the zest of one of the limes.

Once you can mash the sweet potatoes against the side of the pan, the soup is ready. Blitz in the pan using a hand-held blender, until you get a nice smooth consistency. Add the soy sauce, maple syrup and peanut butter and the juice of the zested lime and blitz again to mix. Taste and adjust as needed, adding more lime, soy and maple until it tastes great, you can add a little sea salt here too, if you like. You are aiming for a deeply flavoured soup which balances the sweetness from the potatoes with the earthy peanut butter, and there should be a good back-note of ginger and lime too.

Ladle into bowls, top with the crispy shallots and peanuts and serve with the second lime, cut into wedges, for squeezing over.

Quick saffron polenta bake

Warming saffron-scented polenta is double-cooked here – once in the pan and then finished under the grill with a scattering of tomatoes and feta. The feta crisps and the tomatoes burst as the polenta finishes cooking.

This polenta will be wet, like mashed potato or thick rice pudding, not set, which makes it even more satisfying and comforting.

I love the warming sunny flavour of saffron but it can be pricey. If you don't have any at home, you can make this without it, or use another herb like thyme or oregano. It won't taste the same as the saffron but it will add another dimension to your polenta.

....

Get all your ingredients together and preheat the grill to high.

Put the polenta, saffron and olive oil in the bottom of a deep ovenproof 25cm frying pan over a medium heat. Gradually pour over the stock, beating to prevent lumps. Keep beating until the mixture thickens and starts to bubble, which will take about 5–6 minutes. Season well with salt and pepper.

Shred the spinach and roughly chop the basil, then remove the pan from the heat and stir the spinach and basil into the polenta.

Scatter the tomatoes over the spinach polenta and season well with pepper (no salt if you're using the feta, as it is salty), then crumble over the feta and grate over the zest of the lemon.

Put the pan under the hot grill for 10–12 minutes, until the tomato skins have burst and burnished and the feta has browned and crisped with the heat. Allow to cool for a few minutes before dressing with rocket and pine nuts and serving in the middle of the table for everyone to help themselves.

SERVES 4

150g quick-cook polenta
a good pinch of saffron strands
50ml olive oil
750ml hot vegetable stock
100g spinach
a small bunch of fresh basil
250g cherry tomatoes
100g feta cheese (optional)
1 unwaxed lemon
a handful of rocket, to serve
a handful of toasted pine nuts

Winter root soba noodles with pickled greens

Soba noodles have become a weekly dinner at my house; they are so quick to cook but don't leave you feeling as if you need a lie-down, like a bowl of pasta or more traditional noodles would. I usually mix them with whatever vegetables I have in the fridge, making something fast, fresh, bright and pickled to counter the buckwheat's natural sweetness.

Here I use beets and carrots and make a speedy pickle out of some winter greens, but any quick-cooking veg would do well.

Get all your ingredients together.

Peel the carrot and cut into thin rounds or matchsticks as you like, then do the same with the beetroot. Put a splash of olive oil into a frying pan, then peel and roughly chop the ginger, add to the pan and cook for a minute. Add the carrot and beetroot, a good pinch of salt and about 100ml of water and cook for 5–6 minutes, until all the liquid has evaporated and the carrot and beet have softened.

In the meantime, cook the noodles according to the packet instructions, then drain and cool in cold water.

Shred the greens and mix them with the vinegar, a pinch of salt and 1 teaspoon maple syrup. Scrunch them in your hands for a minute to mix the flavours together.

Once all the water has evaporated from the carrot and beetroot, add the sesame oil, soy or tamari, the other teaspoon of maple syrup, the juice of the lime and the black sesame seeds. Throw in the noodles and toss in the dressing to warm everything through.

Serve the noodles in deep bowls, with the pickled greens and chopped coriander leaves on top, plus some more black sesame seeds and extra limes.

SERVES 2

1 large carrot

1 large beetroot

olive oil

a thumb-size piece of fresh ginger

200g soba noodles
(I use 100% buckwheat ones)

100g kale, chard or spring greens

4 tablespoons brown rice vinegar

2 teaspoons maple syrup

1 teaspoon sesame oil

2 tablespoons soy sauce or tamari

1 lime

1 tablespoon black sesame seeds, plus extra to serve

a small bunch of fresh coriander

Seeded halloumi and harissa rainbow bowl

This is a bowl filled with a few favourite things as well as a killer harissa dressing, burnished seed-encrusted halloumi, my new favourite grain freekeh and of course some avocado. I vary the veg I use here according to the season. I have given you my summer version in the recipe, but below are some ideas for the rest of the year.

> spring – asparagus, peas, spring greens
> summer – tomatoes, yellow beetroots, kale
> autumn – red beetroots, grated carrot, kale
> winter – have a bowl of soup

Freekeh is a type of wheat and means 'rubbed' in Arabic. The story goes that in 2300 BC a shed containing the harvest's young green wheat burnt down. The locals thought the crop was ruined, but they discovered that by rubbing the burnt husk off the wheat it was still edible and in fact toasty and delicious. If you can't get freekeh, any quick-cooking grain like millet or quinoa would work too.

SERVES 4

150g freekeh

coconut oil

300g (or a very big handful) cherry tomatoes

4 beetroots (I use yellow ones)

200g kale (I use purple)

1 lime

1 ripe avocado

200g block of halloumi cheese

2 tablespoons mixed seeds (I used poppy and sesame)

the juice of ½ a lemon

a small bunch of mint

a small bunch of dill

FOR THE DRESSING

a bunch of spring onions

1 teaspoon runny honey

1 tablespoon harissa

2 tablespoons extra virgin olive oil

the juice of ½ a lemon

Weigh out the freekeh in a mug or measuring jug, making a note of the level it comes up to, then put it into a bowl and cover with cold water. Rub the grains in your hands, then drain and wash once more in the same way. Put the freekeh into a pan. Fill the mug or jug to the same level with water and add to the pan, then repeat so you have double the volume of water to freekeh. Add a pinch of salt and a knob of coconut oil, bring to the boil and simmer for 15 minutes until soft but still with a little bite.

Meanwhile, finely slice and fry the spring onions in a little coconut oil until just starting to brown, then scoop them into a jug and add all the other dressing ingredients. Season with salt and pepper and mix well.

Cut the tomatoes in half. Peel the beetroots and use a mandolin or your excellent knife skills to slice them very finely. Remove the stalks and shred

the kale, put into a bowl with the juice of the lime and a pinch of salt and scrunch with your hands for a minute.

Cut the avocado in half and remove the stone, then, with the skin still on, use a small knife to make incisions lengthways along the avocado to form slices.

Put a frying pan on the heat and slice the halloumi thinly. Have your seeds standing by. Put the halloumi into the hot dry pan and cook until brown on one side, which will take about a minute, then flip over and brown the other side. Scatter over the seeds and turn the halloumi in the pan until it is coated with them. Take off the heat.

Once the freekeh is cooked, drain it and dress with the lemon juice, a drizzle of olive oil and a pinch of salt and pepper. Chop the mint and dill and mix through the freekeh.

Serve in shallow bowls, topped with all the rainbow vegetables, the seeded halloumi and generous spoonfuls of the harissa dressing.

Green mimosa salad

My first real job as a chef was at a beautiful local old-world restaurant in Kensington called Daphne's. It was supposed to be Princess Diana's favourite – you get the vibe. Starched tablecloths, Chablis, and charming waiters who had been there so long they had become part of the furniture. It was perfectly calm, pretty posh, with clean, simple salads and pastas.

I worked the starters and pastry sections both at once, quite a baptism of fire. One of the things I remember most was a dressing they made, a mimosa dressing of good Chardonnay vinegar, oil and herbs. Through a hot summer I must have dressed a thousand salads with it. In summer I often crave the simplicity of it on some greens.

I've made this more of a meal, though, by adding eggs. The eggs are mimosa eggs – I've shredded them, which may sound a bit funny at first but it's super-quick and keeps things really light and clean. If you are vegan you can boil and grate in a few potatoes in place of the eggs – it's still delicious.

SERVES 4

6 free-range or organic eggs

500g asparagus

200g broccoli stems
(purple sprouting or Tenderstem)

½ a shallot

2 tablespoons good Chardonnay vinegar (white wine vinegar will do at a pinch)

1 tablespoon extra virgin olive oil

1 tablespoon Dijon mustard

1 ripe avocado

a good bunch of fresh dill
or fennel tops

1 unwaxed lemon

Greek yoghurt or crème fraîche
(optional)

TO SERVE

good rye bread

Fill and boil the kettle and get all your ingredients together.

Put the eggs into a small saucepan and cover them with boiling water from the kettle. Put on a medium heat and bring back to the boil, then simmer for 7 minutes.

Next, snap the tough ends off the asparagus and discard them (you can use them for stock, if you like). Chop the asparagus stems into 1cm rounds, stopping when you get near the top and keeping the tips intact. Chop the broccoli in the same way, stopping when you get close to the floret.

Put the asparagus tips and broccoli florets into a larger saucepan and cover with boiling water. Add a good pinch of salt and simmer for 3 minutes, then add the asparagus and broccoli rounds for a final minute.

Chop the shallot finely and put into a large mixing bowl. Add the vinegar, oil, mustard and a good pinch of salt and pepper and stir to combine.

Once the green vegetables have had their cooking time, drain in a colander and add them to the bowl. While still warm, toss in the dressing. De-stone and cut the avocado into thick slices. Scoop out and add this to the bowl.

Once the eggs are cooked, drain them too and run them under cold water until they are cool enough to handle. Roughly chop the dill or fennel tops. Once the eggs are cool, peel them and grate them into a bowl. Season with salt and pepper, grate over the zest of the lemon, scatter over the dill or fennel and mix gently. If you like, you can add a tablespoon of crème fraîche or Greek yoghurt here.

Serve the veg with spoonfuls of the lemon-and-dill shredded eggs, and a little buttered rye bread if you like (see page 254).

Cashew, kale and lime nacho bowl

Every time I order nachos I am disappointed. They always seem to consist of a pile of over-salted tortilla chips, mountains of rubbery cheese, an afterthought salsa and a scoop of guacamole.

I think nachos deserve more than that, as the layering of flavours and textures in a bowl of nachos has so much potential. Here home-made tortilla chips are topped with crispy lime-spiked kale, a punchy green chilli cashew cream and fresh pops of corn and coriander. There is a little cheese, but if that's not your thing you can skip it, as the nachos will still be flavour-packed.

Here I am not going to recommend using the pure corn tortillas that I usually seek out in Mexican cooking, as they will dry out in the oven; good seeded, wholemeal or gluten-free tortillas work well, as do soft corn tortillas, but be sure to check the back of the pack, as a lot of brands contain unnecessary extras. If you don't recognise what's in them, look elsewhere.

SERVES 4 AS A MEAL
AND 6 AS A SNACK

100g raw unsalted cashews

6 soft wholemeal tortillas
(see note above)

olive or rapeseed oil

½ teaspoon smoked paprika

200g kale

2 limes, unwaxed, plus extra
for serving

2 green chillies

a bunch of fresh coriander

2 corn on the cob

1 ripe avocado

100g good Cheddar
or Manchego cheese

Preheat the oven to 220°C/200°C fan/gas 7. Fill and boil a kettle and get all your ingredients together. Put the cashews into a bowl, cover with boiling water and set aside.

Put your tortillas in a stack and cut them first in half across the middle, then into quarters and then into eighths, so you have tortilla-chip shaped pieces. Put them on to the largest baking tray you have, making sure they don't overlap too much, then drizzle them with a little oil and sprinkle with salt, pepper and some smoked paprika.

De-stem the kale and roughly rip into pieces. Put on another large baking tray, grate over the zest of 1 lime, drizzle over a little oil and sprinkle with salt and pepper.

Put both trays into the oven for 10–15 minutes, until the kale is crisp and the tortillas are nicely browned.

While that is happening, make the cashew cream. You really need a decent blender here, though a hand blender and a deep jug will do. Drain the cashews and put them into the blender with the juice of the zested lime and a good pinch of salt. Roughly chop the green chillies and add to the blender (taking the seeds out if you don't like things super-fiery), and add the stalks from the bunch of coriander too.

Pour in 130ml of water and blitz on high for a couple of minutes, until you have a smooth, grassy green cream. Taste and add more salt, lime and chilli as you need, until it tastes great. If it's looking a bit thick, add another tablespoon of water.

Cut the kernels from the cobs of corn with a sharp knife – I rest the cobs in a mixing bowl while I do this, so the kernels don't go everywhere. De-stone and slice the avo and squeeze over half of the remaining lime.

Once the tortillas and kale are ready, take them out of the oven and turn the grill on to high. Scatter the kale over the tortillas and grate over the cheese. Put the lot under the grill to brown for a couple of minutes, until the cheese is beginning to bubble.

Spoon on the cashew cream, scoop out the avocado and scatter over the corn and coriander leaves. Serve with extra lime wedges for squeezing.

Sesame, pistachio and preserved lemon crispy rice

There is something so satisfying about a simple, well-flavoured pilaf – a pan full of gently but generously spiced rice for dinner. Here I cook the rice for a little longer than you might expect to get a crispy crust on the bottom which is called *tadig* and, to my mind, is the holy grail of rice. If you are in a hurry then you can skip this stage. If you don't have preserved lemon then the zest of a couple of lemons would work well in their place.

Get all your ingredients out and fill and boil a kettle.

Rinse your rice under cold running water for a minute or so then put the rice into a measuring jug and make a note of where it comes up to. Put a pan on a medium heat and add a knob of coconut oil. Once hot, add the rice and fry in the coconut oil for a couple of minutes. Next, fill the measuring jug with the same volume of hot water from the kettle as the rice and add to the pan, then repeat so you have double the amount of water to rice in the pan. Add the saffron and bashed cardamom pods to the pan as well. Put a lid on and cook for 15 minutes, until the rice has absorbed all the water and is fluffy.

While the rice is cooking, toast the sesame seeds and pistachios in a dry frying pan until just browned and fragrant. Halve the preserved lemons and scoop out the middles and discard, then finely chop the rind. Remove the seeds from the pomegranate. I do this by cutting it in half and holding one half, cut-side down, in my hand over a bowl and tapping with a wooden spoon so that the seeds fall out. Chop the parsley and dill leaves. Mix the yoghurt with the juice and zest of the lemon and the herbs and season well.

Once the rice is ready, make three holes in it and add a little more coconut oil to each, put on a high heat for 8 minutes so that the rice crisps up at the bottom. Once crispy, take off the heat and spoon onto a platter. Mix with the nuts, seeds, preserved lemon and pomegranate seeds. Serve generous bowls of the rice topped with the herbed yoghurt and some rocket or watercress.

SERVES 4

150g brown basmati rice
a knob of coconut oil
a good pinch of saffron
6 cardamom pods
4 tablespoons sesame seeds
(about 30g)
50g pistachios
4 preserved lemons
1 pomegranate

TO SERVE
a small bunch of parsley
a small bunch of dill
100ml yoghurt
1 unwaxed lemon
a couple of handfuls of rocket
or watercress

Black-eyed beans with chard and green herb smash

This is a super-quick stew which has its roots in Palestine. Pick your chard colour here – the clean green Swiss or the sweet-shop neon Bright Lights chard. It is not often that one vegetable provides such a rainbow of options.

Black-eyed beans were often overlooked in my kitchen in favour of earthy black beans, buttery cannellini or plump butter beans. No longer though, as black-eyed beans are a new favourite. Sometimes, I like to top this with tahini for an extra layer of flavour.

....

Fill and boil a kettle and get all your ingredients together. Put a large saucepan on the heat.

Wash and finely slice the leek. Add to the saucepan with a tablespoon of coconut or olive oil and cook for a couple of minutes until soft and sweet. Finely slice the garlic and add to the pan with the chilli powder or dried chilli and cook for a couple of minutes, until the garlic is beginning to brown. Add the black-eyed beans with their liquid, the stock powder or cube and 200ml of hot water from the kettle and bring to a simmer. Grate in the nutmeg, squeeze in the juice of half the lemon, add the squeezed lemon half to the pan and simmer for 10 minutes or so. Meanwhile, strip the leaves from the chard stalks. Finely slice the stalks and add them to the pan, then finely shred the leaves and put to one side.

Put all the ingredients for the herb smash into a food processor and blitz until you have a smooth grassy paste. Season well with salt and pepper.

Once the black beans are soft and flavourful and the liquid has reduced to a thick soup-like consistency, stir in the chard leaves, season well with salt and pepper and leave to cook for a couple of minutes. Scoop into deep bowls and spoon over the herb smash. If you're really hungry, some rice or flatbread would go well.

SERVES 4

FOR THE BEANS
1 leek
1 tablespoon coconut oil or olive oil
2 cloves of garlic
a good pinch of chilli powder or chopped dried chilli
2 × 400g tins of black-eyed beans
1 teaspoon vegetable stock powder, or ½ a stock cube
a good grating of nutmeg
½ an unwaxed lemon
200g bunch of Swiss or rainbow chard

FOR THE HERB SMASH
a large bunch of fresh coriander
2 green chillies
2 cloves of garlic
30g shelled walnuts
1 tablespoon runny honey or maple syrup
2 tablespoons good olive oil
the juice of ½ a lemon

Crispy cauliflower rice with sticky spiced cashews

There is something so subtle and even-tempered about cauliflower. I love to eat it two ways. To highlight its gentleness with subtle bay and cheeses or to go to the other extreme and hit it with punchy spices and serious flavour – cauliflower holds on to flavour so well.

Here I make rice out of the cauliflower, which has become quite a thing among healthy eaters. It's often eaten raw, which I have to say isn't for me. Instead I sauté it so it's browned and crispy-edged, and spike it with my favourite southern Indian duo: mustard seeds and curry leaves. It's topped with some freshness from radishes and a crunch from spiced cashews. A dish that sits firmly at the crossroads of healthy and delicious.

If you can't find curry leaves, just leave them out, as I am yet to find an alternative flavour match. I have also made this using broccoli, which is equally delicious.

I suggest using coconut nectar here to sweeten. Coconut nectar is the nutrient-rich sap of the coconut tree. It's harvested by tapping into the tree to release the sap, much like maple syrup. It's packed with nutrients and amino acids and is low GI, so it won't spike your blood sugar like normal sugar. I use it anywhere I need a bit of sweetness.

....

Get all your ingredients together and set up your food processor.

Take the leaves and gnarly root off your cauliflower and chop it into big chunks. Put them into the food processor and pulse until you have a rice-like texture.

Put your largest frying pan on a high heat (if you don't have a nice big one, two smaller ones will work). Peel and finely slice the onion and add to the pan with a large knob of coconut oil. Cook for 5 minutes, until soft, stirring from time to time. Meanwhile, roughly chop the garlic and

SERVES 4

1 medium cauliflower (about 600g)
1 red onion
a large knob of coconut oil
2 cloves of garlic
a thumb-size piece of fresh ginger
1 tablespoon black mustard seeds
a large handful of fresh curry leaves
100g cashew nuts
a small bunch of radishes
a small bunch of fresh coriander
a couple of handfuls of pea shoots or dainty salad leaves
a squeeze of coconut nectar or honey
a pinch of garam masala
zest and juice of 1 unwaxed lime

TO SERVE (OPTIONAL)
4 chapattis or roti
a little lime pickle or mango chutney

ginger. Once the onion is soft, add the garlic and ginger, the mustard seeds and curry leaves and cook for a couple of minutes, then season well with sea salt.

Now turn the heat right up. Add the cauliflower rice and cook, stirring every couple of minutes to make sure all the rice gets a little browned on the bottom of the pan – this will take about 10 minutes.

Meanwhile, in another dry frying pan toast the cashews until just brown. Thinly slice the radishes, pick the coriander leaves from their stalks and mix both with the pea shoots or salad leaves.

When the cashews are toasted, toss them with a little coconut nectar or honey and a pinch of garam masala and take off the heat.

As soon as the cauliflower rice is nicely browned all over, spoon it on to a platter. Crumble over the cashews, scatter over the salad, grate over the zest of the lime and squeeze over the juice. If you are really hungry you could serve it with some chapattis or roti, and a little lime pickle or mango chutney.

Courgetti with pistachio, green herbs and ricotta

I resisted including a recipe for these vegetable noodles, as they are on every scene-y or healthy menu and are peppered through raw and healthy cookbooks. But the fact is they are quick and simple and I love eating them. I am not going to insist that you go out and buy a spiraliser if you don't have one; I do have one, but still often use a speed-peeler and a knife rather than getting out this gadget. A julienne peeler, which costs a couple of pounds, will do exactly the same job and take up much less cupboard space.

Vegans, either leave out the ricotta or you can bake silken tofu in the same way, if you like.

Preheat the oven to 200°C/180°C fan/gas 6. Fill and boil a kettle and get all your ingredients together.

Turn the ricotta out of its packet on to a baking tray, grate over the zest of one lemon, sprinkle over a large pinch of dried chilli and drizzle over the honey. Put the ricotta into the oven to bake for 15 minutes, until caramelised on top.

Put the pistachios into the oven to toast for 3–5 minutes. Heat a frying pan on a high heat and thinly slice one of the unzested lemons, picking out and discarding any pips. Add a tablespoon of olive oil to the pan and fry the lemon slices until they are burnished and sticky.

Take the pistachios out of the oven and tumble into the bowl of your food processor and pick the mint and basil leaves in too. Add the juice of half the zested lemon and a good pinch of salt. Add 4 tablespoons of olive oil and a tablespoon of cold water, pulse until you have a textured grassy green pesto, then transfer to a bowl.

Now for the courgettes. Use a julienne peeler or a spiraliser if you have one to make courgette noodles. To do this by hand, use a speed-peeler

SERVES 4

250g ricotta cheese
3 unwaxed lemons
a good pinch of dried chilli flakes
1 teaspoon runny honey
60g shelled pistachios
extra virgin olive oil
a small bunch of fresh mint
a small bunch of fresh basil
4 large or 6 small courgettes

Courgetti with pistachio, green herbs
and ricotta

or a mandolin to peel the courgettes into long thin strips. Carefully stack
the slices on top of each other and use a knife to cut them into thin strips.
This is actually really easy and quick, so don't be put off. Place in a heatproof
mixing bowl, cover with boiling water from the kettle and leave to sit
for 2–3 minutes.

Once the fried lemon slices are cool enough to handle, roughly chop them
and stir them through the pesto. Remove the ricotta from the oven.

Drain the courgetti well and toss with the pesto. Crumble over the ricotta
and finish with more lemon zest and a drizzle of oil, if you like.

Charred broccoli with cucumber noodles and peanut sauce

This bowl of freshness and flavour is half based on a banging bowl of dan dan noodles I ate in LA and half based on a charred cauliflower I made a couple of weeks later. I wanted to put the charred smokiness and the peanutty sweetness in one bowl.

Instead of using normal noodles here I've made some quick cucumber noodles with a speed-peeler – they add an amazing freshness and work brilliantly as a foil to the charred smoky broccoli and richly fragrant peanut sauce. If I am really hungry I serve this with a pile of jasmine rice or noodles.

When you're buying peanut butter be sure to check the ingredients list – it should have nothing apart from peanuts and perhaps a little salt. If it has anything else, put it back. I use crunchy here but smooth would work too; I'll leave that up to your own peanut butter leanings. See page 226 for my nut butter recipes.

When you are making the cucumber noodles you'll be left with the middle of the cucumbers. I usually chop them up and use them to infuse my drinking water in the fridge, but sometimes I blitz the middle bits and freeze them in ice cubes for a cucumber-iced gin and tonic. Seriously good.

....

Fill and boil a kettle and get all your ingredients together.

Trim the broccoli and make an incision down each stalk to help them cook quicker. If you are using normal broccoli, cut the bottom of the stem off and slice into long thin trees. Put the trimmed broccoli into a bowl and cover with boiling water from the kettle. Leave for 5 minutes, then drain and set aside.

Meanwhile, get a small pan on the heat and add a knob of coconut oil. Finely slice the garlic and, once the oil is hot, add to the pan. Fry for a couple of minutes until just crisp, being careful not to burn, then drain on kitchen paper.

SERVES 4

FOR THE BROCCOLI
400g purple sprouting broccoli, or 1 large head of normal broccoli
a knob of coconut oil
3 cloves of garlic
3 cucumbers
1 tablespoon runny honey
1 tablespoon tamari or light soy sauce
1 red chilli
1 tablespoon sesame oil
1 unwaxed lime

FOR THE PEANUT GINGER SAUCE
6 tablespoons good peanut butter
a thumb-size piece of fresh ginger
2 tablespoons rice wine vinegar
the zest and juice of 1 unwaxed lime
1 tablespoon tamari or soy sauce
1 tablespoon maple syrup

Next, get on with the cucumber noodles. Use a normal speed-peeler to peel each side of the cucumber into thin ribbons, stopping when you get to the watery middle bit, which doesn't make good noodles and discarding the peel if you like. (See introduction for suggestions about what to do with the leftover middles.) Put a griddle on a high heat to heat up.

Now for the peanut sauce. Whisk the peanut butter with 100ml of warm water, then peel and grate in the ginger, add all the other sauce ingredients and mix well. Add a little water if needed, you are after double cream consistency.

Toss the broccoli with the honey and soy. Chop the red chilli and add to the broccoli along with the sesame oil. Place on the griddle and cook for a couple of minutes on each side, until nicely charred.

Divide the cucumber noodles between your bowls and top with the peanut sauce, broccoli and crispy garlic. Finish with the zest of a lime, then cut the lime into wedges and serve on the side.

Quinoa risotto with mashed peas and greens

I feel a bit bad calling this a risotto really. I spent a good year in the kitchen of Fifteen mastering a perfect risotto surrounded by brilliant Italian cooks: the stirring, the creaminess, the perfect rice, the resting, the butter and Parmesan. But the reality is, I don't want risotto every day. This is more my style on a weeknight – it's got the warming, hearty, nurturing feeling that I love in a risotto, topped with the freshness of a quick sweet pea smash, greens and lots of heady fresh herbs.

In winter I make this with mashed roast carrots or beetroots in place of the peas and some flash-fried winter greens; the fresh green herbs are replaced with thyme and rosemary oil. Equally delicious.

....

Fill and boil a kettle and get all your ingredients together.

Wash and finely slice the leeks. Heat a pan and add a couple of tablespoons of olive oil. Add the leeks and cook until beginning to brown, then finely slice the garlic, add to the pan and cook for a minute or two.

Meanwhile, add the quinoa and cook for a few minutes, allowing it to pop and crackle and toast; this will give it a much better flavour. Once you've had a few minutes of crackling, add the white wine and the juice of half the lemon and cook until the wine has evaporated. Add the stock powder or cube and 600ml of boiling water and bring to a gentle simmer.

Weigh out the peas into a measuring jug and cover with boiling water from the kettle to defrost them. Shred the greens finely and put to one side. Toast the pine nuts in a dry pan until just browned.

Drain the defrosted peas and put into the bowl of a blender. Pick the mint and basil leaves from the stalks and add to the bowl with a good pinch of salt, the juice of the other half lemon and 1 tablespoon of olive oil and blitz until smooth.

SERVES 4

2 leeks

olive oil

2 cloves of garlic

250g quinoa

200ml white wine

1 lemon

1 tablespoon of vegetable stock powder, or ½ a stock cube

250g frozen peas

200g spring greens or spinach

50g pine nuts

a few sprigs of fresh mint

½ a bunch of fresh basil

60g Parmesan cheese (I use a vegetarian one)

100g ricotta or feta cheese (optional)

When the quinoa is the consistency of loose porridge, pop a lid on and keep on a low heat. Add the shredded greens and stir through the quinoa, adding a little more boiling water if you need to, to get it to a loose risotto consistency. Grate in the Parmesan and stir through. Season well with black pepper – you won't need much salt, as the stock will be salty.

Serve the quinoa topped with the pea mash, some toasted pine nuts, the crumbled ricotta or feta, if using, and a final grating of Parmesan.

Beetroot and buckwheat pancakes

The buckwheat and beetroot make these pancakes more satisfying and hearty than a normal one. If you can't get buckwheat flour, spelt or wholemeal will do in its place.

This is a brilliantly vibrant dinner of reds, greens, oranges and golden browns, and it looks so pretty on the plate. You can make the pancakes with carrots instead, in which case they are best topped with almonds and lime zest.

Get all your ingredients and equipment together.

Put the buckwheat flour and baking powder into a bowl and whisk in first 250ml of the milk and then the egg (if you are using chia seeds, add those instead of the egg, along with 3 tablespoons of cold water). Add a pinch of salt and grate in the beetroot using a fine grater. Leave the batter to sit while you get on with a few other things. It will thicken while it sits. You're after a thick, American pancake batter consistency. You can add a little more milk if you need to.

Heat a pan on a high heat, add the hazelnuts and toast until golden brown. Put to one side. De-stone the olives. Put the pan back on the heat, add a teaspoon of coconut oil, then the olives. Fry until they are beginning to crisp, then take them out of the pan and put aside for later.

Now back to the pancakes. Put the pan back on the heat and add a little more coconut oil. Once hot, add 2 tablespoons of the batter to make little Scotch-sized pancakes, fitting as many into the pan as you can. Cook for 2–3 minutes, until bubbles appear on the top and they are starting to crisp up around the sides, then flip and cook on the other side for 1–2 minutes. Keep warm while you make the rest. If you are in a hurry you can have two pans on the go.

Once the pancakes are all cooked, pile them on to four plates and top them with a little goat's curd or cheese, the toasted hazelnuts, a shock of greens, the crisped olives and a grating of orange zest.

SERVES 4
(MAKES 12 PANCAKES)

250g buckwheat flour

1 heaped teaspoon baking powder

250–300ml unsweetened almond milk or normal milk

1 free-range or organic egg, or 1 tablespoon chia seeds

1 medium beetroot, peeled

50g blanched hazelnuts

100g black olives

coconut oil

125g goat's curd or soft goat's cheese

4 small handfuls of green salad leaves

1 unwaxed orange

quick 20-minute stir-fries

Follow this formula each time: Main veg, Back-up veg, Protein, Aromatics, Rice/noodles, Seasoning/dressing, Crunch.

You'll need a good wok and to have all your ingredients chopped before you start. Make sure you get your wok or pan screaming hot. Always start by adding the vegetables that will take the longest to cook. Fry for a couple of minutes, turning all the time, then add the remaining vegetables and the protein. Cook until just beginning to brown, then add the aromatics (if you add them at the beginning they'll burn), your cooked rice or noodles and, finally, any dressing. Add the crunch once scooped into bowls.

MAIN VEG →	BACK-UP VEG →	PROTEIN →
BROCCOLI	GREENS	TOFU
SWEET POTATO	BROCCOLI PAK CHOI	TEMPEH
SQUASH	SUGAR SNAPS SPINACH	SEITAN
CABBAGE	CARROTS	PANEER
GREENS	SPRING ONIONS BEANSPROUTS	EGG (BEATEN)
MUSHROOMS	MANGETOUT GREENS	TOFU

AROMATICS	→	RICE/ NOODLES	→	SEASONING/ DRESSING	→	CRUNCH
GINGER CHILLI GARLIC		JASMINE RICE		SESAME OIL SOY SAUCE		SESAME SEEDS
GINGER GARLIC		SOBA NOODLES		MISO LIME MAPLE SYRUP		BLACK SESAME SEEDS
GINGER GARLIC SPRING ONIONS		BROWN RICE		SESAME OIL RICE WINE MAPLE SYRUP		CASHEWS
GINGER CHILLI GARLIC		BASMATI RICE		MUSTARD SEEDS HONEY		TOASTED FLAKED ALMONDS
GINGER CHILLI GARLIC		FLAT RICE NOODLES		SOY SAUCE SESAME OIL CHILLI SAUCE		ROASTED PEANUTS
GINGER CHILLI		EGG NOODLES		LIME		

on the
table
in half
an hour

A lot can happen in half an hour, this is still quick cooking but with an opportunity to layer flavour with more subtlety. Quinoa cakes, chickpea pancakes, butternut hash, black bean fritters, greens-stuffed burritos, sweet roast courgette ratatouille, killer chilli, speedy spelt pizza, deep and moreish chowder and sticky sweet chilli paneer.

25 MINUTES

Carrot and chickpea pancake with lemon-spiked dressing

This is a light but hearty pancake made from chickpea flour and grated carrots. I made these a lot while staying with my sister in California, and they are what Californian cooking is all about for me – delicious, nourishing, light and bright. Chickpea flour is cheap and easy to find; it will be in the Indian section at the supermarket and may be called gram flour.

The batter can be easily doubled or tripled for more pancakes. It keeps well in the fridge until the next day, if necessary, though you may need to loosen it to pancake-batter consistency with a little more water or milk. For a vegan version, make the sauce using soaked and blitzed cashews in place of the cottage cheese.

SERVES 2

FOR THE PANCAKE

150g chickpea flour

230ml milk of your choice
(I use unsweetened almond)

2 tablespoons extra virgin olive oil

2 medium carrots

ghee or coconut oil

FOR THE SAUCE

8 cornichons

1 green chilli

a few sprigs of fresh parsley

a few sprigs of fresh dill

4 tablespoons cottage cheese
or Greek yoghurt

½ tablespoon vegetarian
Worcestershire sauce

a splash of chilli sauce

the zest of ½ an unwaxed lemon

TO SERVE

a couple of handfuls of sprouted
seeds and pulses

a few handfuls of baby salad leaves

First, make your batter. In a large bowl, sift the chickpea flour and add a generous pinch of salt and freshly ground black pepper. Whisk in the almond milk and olive oil and let the mixture sit, covered, while you make your sauce.

Finely chop the cornichons and the green chilli. Chop the leaves of the parsley and dill. Put all this into a small bowl with the cottage cheese, Worcestershire sauce, chilli sauce and lemon zest. Mix well and season with salt and pepper to taste.

Peel and grate the carrots and stir them into the batter. Place a large non-stick frying pan on a high heat and add a teaspoon of ghee or coconut oil. Add the batter and allow it to cook for 4–5 minutes, until the pancake is set around the edges and starting to brown and crisp. Place a plate on top of the pancake then cover your hand with a tea towel and flip the pancake onto the plate. Slide off the plate back into the pan and cook on the other side for 4–5 minutes.

Cut the pancake into slices and top with sprouted seeds, salad leaves and spoonfuls of the sauce.

Squash, greens and quinoa fritters and sumac yoghurt

These fritters are hearty without leaving you feeling groaningly full.

Don't be tempted to skip the lemon and sumac yoghurt, as it really makes these little cakes sing. I like to use a mixture of different-coloured quinoa here, as it adds to the beauty of the green and sunset-orange-flecked fritters. The mixture keeps well in the fridge if you want to cook them as you go, and the cooked fritters keep for a couple of days in the fridge – they are great torn into a flatbread with some leaves for lunch or in a good bun instead of a burger.

To make this vegan, use silken tofu in place of the feta and 4 tablespoons of chia seeds soaked to a gel in 12 tablespoons of water to replace the eggs, and be more generous with the seasoning.

....

Fill and boil a kettle and get all your ingredients and equipment together.

If you are cooking the quinoa, weigh it out into a mug, noting the level it comes up to, quickly rinse under cold water, then pour it into a pan. Fill the mug to the same level with water and add to the pan, then repeat so you have double the volume of water to quinoa. Bring to the boil, then turn down the heat and simmer for about 10–12 minutes, until almost all the water has been absorbed and the little curly grain has been released from each quinoa seed.

Meanwhile, peel, deseed and grate the squash and add it to the quinoa (the squash doesn't need to be submerged, it can steam on top of the quinoa). Simmer for the last 2–3 minutes of the quinoa's cooking time, until it has lost its rawness and is mushy. Drain, if there is any water remaining, then put back on the heat and cook for a couple of minutes to get rid of all the moisture – you should hear a crackle. Spread out on a baking tray to cool quickly.

SERVES 4 (MAKES 8 FRITTERS)

a mugful of uncooked red, white or black quinoa (about 150g), or 2 mugfuls of cooked quinoa (about 300g)

a 400g piece of butternut squash

a bunch of spring onions

200g fresh greens (spinach, kale or chard)

60g rolled oats

1 teaspoon toasted cumin seeds

200g feta cheese

1 unwaxed lemon

4 medium free-range or organic eggs

a small bunch of fresh parsley

a small bunch of fresh coriander

extra virgin olive oil

FOR THE YOGHURT

150ml yoghurt of your choice (I use good Greek or coconut)

1 teaspoon sumac or dried chilli

TO SERVE

½ a cucumber

4 ripe tomatoes

a handful of good black olives

4 handfuls of salad leaves

Finely chop the spring onions and shred the greens. Place in a large mixing bowl with the oats and cumin. Crumble in the feta, then add some salt, freshly ground black pepper and the zest of the lemon and mix well. Add the cooled quinoa (it can still be slightly warm) and the eggs, then roughly chop and stir in the herbs. Mix well and put into the fridge while you get on with another couple of jobs.

Use this time to get your salad ready: peel, deseed and slice the cucumber, slice the tomatoes and de-stone the olives. Mix the lot with the juice of half the zested lemon, a drizzle of olive oil and season with salt and freshly ground black pepper. Divide the leaves between four bowls and top with the tomato mixture.

Mix the yoghurt with some sea salt and the juice of the other half of the lemon, then stir in the sumac or chilli.

Take the quinoa mixture out of the fridge and mould into eight rough patties with your hands. Heat the oil in a frying pan on a medium heat. Add the patties and fry for about 4 minutes on each side, until golden brown.

Serve the fritters with generous spoonfuls of the yoghurt and salad.

35 MINUTES

Bloody Mary salad with black rice

Black rice is also magically known as forbidden rice. It's dense and moreish, and cooked this way it has a comforting starchiness which is offset by the bloody Mary-dressed tomatoes and some quick pickled onions. If you have lovage growing in your garden or see it in your local shop it would be a brilliant addition here, but for most people it's hard to find, so I've left it out.

Black rice is cultivated in Asia and is my new favourite. It's usually unmilled, with the fibre-rich black husks still intact. It is this outer layer that sets black rice apart from other types of unmilled rice, as the deep, dark pigments it contains boast special nutrients, the same ones you find in antioxidant-rich black grapes and blueberries. As it is unmilled it takes longer to cook than white rice.

In the winter I eat this black rice with roasted beetroots in place of the tomatoes. The colours are amazing deep hues of winter.

If you have time, soak the rice overnight in double the amount of cold water; if not, don't sweat, it will just take a little longer to cook. By celery heart I mean just the centre few stalks of the celery, the point at which they turn more yellow than green. If you are using jarred horseradish, try to search out the pure grated stuff, which is stronger and hasn't been mixed into a horseradish sauce or cream.

....

Get all your ingredients together and boil the kettle.

Rinse the rice under cold running water. Place it in a saucepan with 1 litre of hot water, cover with a lid, bring to the boil, then lower the heat and cook gently for about 30 minutes (or up to 50 minutes if it is unsoaked), or until the rice is tender and all the water has been absorbed.

SERVES 4

250g black rice

1 small red onion

3 tablespoons sherry or red wine vinegar

500g different-coloured tomatoes

1 celery heart

100g fat black olives

2 tablespoons extra virgin olive oil

1 tablespoon vegetarian Worcestershire sauce

1 teaspoon Tabasco or similar chilli sauce

2 tablespoons freshly grated or jarred horseradish

1 lemon

Finely slice the red onion, then put it into a bowl with a tablespoon of the vinegar and a good pinch of salt and give it all a good scrunch to help it pickle.

Chop the tomatoes into shapes and sizes that make the most of their own individual beauty. Very finely slice the celery (keeping the inner leaves for later), de-stone and roughly chop the olives and put everything into a big bowl.

Now make your dressing. Mix the oil and the remaining 2 tablespoons of vinegar in a little bowl, then add the Worcestershire sauce and Tabasco and pour over the tomato mixture. Season the lot with some more salt and pepper, grate or scatter over the horseradish, toss together and leave to one side for the flavours to develop.

Once the rice is cooked, drain any excess water (there may not be any if you measured spot on) and season with salt and pepper. Squeeze over the juice of the lemon. The rice will be thick and sticky, a bit like black rice pudding, but should loosen a little once the lemon has been stirred in. Spoon the rice on to a platter, top with the onions, then the tomatoes and, finally, scatter over the celery leaves. I serve this with a simple rocket or watercress salad.

Black bean and corn fritters

These cumin-spiked fritters are super-quick and easy. They are made with ingredients I almost always have to hand and, in a fix, tinned, unsweetened corn would work too.

The avocado smash I make to go with these fritters is spiked with three types of citrus, which makes it super-refreshing. I chop the citrus whole, which works so well, just take care to cut away any pith, and make sure you cut out the pithy bit in the middle too. If you are in a hurry, just use the zest and a little juice instead. I like to serve this with a lime-dressed green salad. These fritters are also great torn up like falafel in flatbreads with crunchy lettuce and hummus.

....

Preheat the oven to 180°C/160°C fan/gas 4. Get all your ingredients together.

Shred the spinach or greens and put into a large mixing bowl. Drain the beans and add to the bowl. Use a fork to mash the beans a little.

Cut the corn from the cob – when I do this I put it into a bowl and carefully cut the kernels off with a knife so they don't fly everywhere. Add the corn kernels to the beans and greens.

Finely chop the chilli and coriander – stalks and all – and add most of this to the bowl. Crack in the eggs. Season generously with salt and pepper.

Heat a dry frying pan and toast the cumin seeds for 30 seconds or so, then add these to the bowl too. Give it all a good mix.

Heat a little coconut oil in the pan. Take heaped tablespoonfuls of the mixture and add them to the pan 3–4 at a time. You should get about 8 fritters. Fry for a couple of minutes until golden brown on the bottom and set and golden around the edges before flipping over. Once the first lot are cooked,

SERVES 4
(MAKES 8 FRITTERS)

200g spinach or greens
1 × 400g tin of black beans
2 corn on the cob
1 red chilli
a small bunch of fresh coriander
4 free-range or organic eggs
a good pinch of cumin seeds
coconut oil

FOR THE AVOCADO SMASH
2 ripe avocados
1 lime
1 lemon
1 orange

place them on a large baking tray and pop them into the oven to keep warm while you cook the remaining fritters.

While the fritters are cooking, mash the avocados with a little salt and pepper. Use a knife to cut the peel from each of the citrus fruits. Cut each one into quarters, then cut out the pithy middle and roughly chop the fruit, removing any big bits of pith. Add to the avocado with the rest of the chilli and coriander and mix well.

Serve the fritters topped with the smashed avocado and some green salad.

Butternut and sweet leek hash

This is my dream brunch. I can't get enough of it. So much so that I make it for lunch and dinner as well. Most Sunday nights when I was growing up, dinner would be Dad's fry-up – not the bacon and egg kind, but all our Sunday veg crisped up to within an inch of its life, that amazing golden stuff that happens on the bottom of a pan.

It is a pan full of good things: burnished squash, sweet caramel leeks, golden potatoes and perfect sunshine eggs, topped off with a neat little herb and leek dressing that takes this hash to the next level. Though my dad would probably still have a spoonful of Branston pickle on the side.

This all happens in half an hour in the pan. It's also a great way to use up leftover cooked root vegetables, which would make it even quicker.
If you are vegan, skip the cheese and eggs and use 100g of soaked cashews blitzed with 100ml of cold water in place of the yoghurt. I make this for my family a lot and it's really good this way too.

....

Fill and boil a kettle and get your ingredients together. Put a large non-stick pan on a medium heat.

Wash the leeks, then finely shred them and add them to the pan with a little of the coconut oil. Stir every couple of minutes.

While the leeks are cooking, cut the potatoes into 1cm pieces and put them into a large saucepan. Pour over boiling water from the kettle and bring to the boil, then turn down the heat and simmer for 5 minutes.

Deseed the squash and cut into pieces about the same size as the potatoes. Once the potatoes have had 5 minutes, add the squash to the pan of boiling water for a final 3 minutes of cooking. Once the potatoes and squash have had their time and have softened a little, drain them and leave in the colander to steam dry a little.

SERVES 2, OR 4 WITH EGGS

2 leeks

1 tablespoon coconut or olive oil

400g new potatoes

½ a medium butternut squash

a few fresh chives

a few sprigs of fresh parsley

4 tablespoons crème fraîche or yoghurt

½ a lemon

a crumble of Lancashire or Cheddar cheese (optional)

4 free-range or organic eggs (optional)

Spoon 3 tablespoons of the leeks into a deep bowl or jug. Turn the heat up under the leek pan, add a little more oil if necessary, then add the potatoes and squash and fry, turning every couple of minutes, but not too often – you want to allow each side enough time to build up a bit of a golden crust.

Chop the herbs and add them to the reserved 3 tablespoons of leeks. Add the crème fraîche or yoghurt, the juice of half a lemon and some salt and pepper, and blitz well, using a hand-held blender.

Keep turning the hash in the pan until it's all nicely golden. Now there are a couple of ways you can take it. Keep it like this – it's delicious as it is. Or crumble a little cheese over and allow it to melt in. Then crack 4 eggs into the pan, pop a lid on top and allow to cook for 3–5 minutes, until the whites are set but the yolks are still runny.

Serve the hash with the leek and herb dressing scattered over. Be sure to stir it through before you eat.

30-minute sweet potato chilli

Usually the joy of chilli is that it has been blipping away on the hob building up flavour for hours, but this chilli is different. It's a bit fresher and brighter, but it's still packed with flavour from the chipotle and spices and is topped with a bright chilli and herb drizzle. A pot of this will keep a houseful happy for a couple of nights – or it will freeze and feed a few dinners for two.

Get all your ingredients together and put a large saucepan and a frying pan on a medium heat.

Empty the passata, lentils, beans and quinoa into the saucepan and add 400ml of cold water. Add the chipotle and cook on the highest heat for 10–15 minutes.

Peel, quarter and finely slice the sweet potato, roughly slice the spring onions and peel the garlic. Put the spring onions and sweet potato into the frying pan with a little coconut or olive oil and fry for 5 minutes. Add the smoked paprika and fry for a further 3 minutes.

Using a fine grater, grate the cloves of garlic into the tomato quinoa mixture with the cumin and coriander and stir in.

Take a ladleful of chilli out of the saucepan and add it to the sweet potatoes in the frying pan. Swill the whole lot around to get the goodness from the bottom of the pan, then pour it all carefully into the chilli pan. Simmer together for another 10 minutes with a lid on. Drain the red peppers, roughly slice them and add them to the chilli pan.

While the chilli is cooking, put the green chilli and coriander into a blender with the oregano or thyme, the juice of the lime and 2 tablespoons of olive oil. Add 4 tablespoons of water and a pinch of salt and blitz until smooth.

Serve the chilli in deep bowls, topped with yoghurt and the chilli drizzle.

SERVES 6

1 × 750ml jar of passata
1 × 400g tin of Puy lentils
1 × 400g tin of aduki beans
50g quinoa
1–2 tablespoons chipotle paste
(depending on how hot you like things)
1 large sweet potato
a bunch of spring onions
(about 125g)
2 cloves of garlic
coconut or olive oil
1 tablespoon smoked paprika
1 tablespoon ground cumin
1 tablespoon ground coriander
1 × 220g jar of roasted red peppers

TO SERVE

1–2 deseeded green chillies
a bunch of fresh coriander
a few sprigs of fresh oregano or thyme
1 lime
extra virgin olive oil
coconut yoghurt or good
Greek yoghurt

Persian pea and herb little bakes with beetroot labneh

I love the Persian way of eating: the spices, the sharing and the sense of family. One of my best friends, Mersedeh, is from a family of incredible Persian cooks and I remember eating these little bakes, *kookoo shabzi*, a generously herbed kind of Persian frittata, at their family parties. I get my fix of these now at a great Persian stall on Broadway Market in Hackney, where kookoos are made in dainty little portions.

These are my version. I expect they veer a long way from the original (especially with the addition of peas), but they are my homage to Persian food and family in all its colourful, highly flavoured glory. I've been told the key to a good *kookoo shabzi* is to use an equal amount of each herb so the flavours are balanced, and to gently cook the herbs first to release all their water. I serve them with a beetroot labneh (salted yoghurt) and some leaves and flatbreads.

I have purposely planned this recipe so that you have a few of these little kookoos left over, as I want you to try how great they are thrown into a wrap with some pickles and a drizzle of tahini for lunch the next day.

SERVES 4

FOR THE BAKES
a good pinch of saffron strands
400g frozen peas
4 spring onions
a bunch of fresh mint
a bunch of fresh dill
a bunch of fresh chives
a bunch of fresh parsley
a little olive oil
1 heaped teaspoon ground coriander
6 free-range or organic eggs
1 green chilli

FOR THE BEETROOT LABNEH
2 small cooked beetroots
8 tablespoons good, thick Greek yoghurt
1 tablespoon tahini
1 unwaxed lemon
a small handful of walnuts

Preheat the oven to 220°C/200°C fan/gas 7. Fill and boil a kettle and get all your ingredients and equipment together. Put a non-stick frying pan on the heat. You'll also need a non-stick 12-hole muffin tin.

Once the kettle has boiled, soak the saffron in a little boiling water (about 25ml). Put the peas into a heatproof bowl and cover with more boiling water.

Finely chop the spring onions, then finely chop all the herbs to a more or less even size. Heat a little oil in the hot frying pan and add the onions, all but a little pinch of the herbs and all the ground coriander. Stir for 1–2 minutes, until softened and wilted.

Whisk the eggs in a large mixing jug or bowl, then add the saffron liquid, drained peas and the wilted herbs and spring onions. Chop the chilli finely and add that too, season with sea salt and black pepper. Mix well.

Drizzle a tiny bit of oil into each hole of a 12-hole muffin tin and jiggle it around a bit to coat the holes. Pop the muffin tin into the oven for 30 seconds for the oil to warm up. Then take the tin out of the oven and pour the batter into each hole, to come two-thirds of the way up. Place in the hot oven for 10–12 minutes, until cooked through and slightly golden.

While the bakes are cooking, grate the beetroots into a bowl. Add the yoghurt, a really good pinch of salt, the tahini and the juice and zest of the lemon, mix well, then break over the walnuts and scatter the remaining herbs over the top.

Serve two bakes each, with warm flatbreads, salad leaves and generous spoonfuls of the beetroot labneh.

Squash, roast tomato and popped black bean salad

This salad is all about texture; not that it doesn't taste fantastic, but texture is one of the things I think we often forget about when we are putting a meal together. Here it's crisp roast squash slices, soft roast tomatoes and popped black beans, which add an amazingly crunchy, almost popcorn, element.

....

Preheat the oven to 240°C/220°C fan/gas 9 and get all your ingredients together.

Halve and deseed your squash and cut it into 1cm slices. Place them on a baking tray and drizzle with a little oil, then sprinkle with salt, pepper and the ground cardamom seeds. Place in the hot oven for 25 minutes, until blistered and golden, turning halfway through cooking.

Halve the cherry tomatoes and put them on another tray. Grate over the ginger and season with salt and pepper. Drizzle over a little oil and put into the oven with the squash; your tomatoes will take about 20 minutes.

Meanwhile, drain your black beans well and dry them on kitchen paper. Heat a large pan on a medium heat, and once it's nice and hot add the beans and dry fry, turning from time to time, until they pop and turn crisp.

When the time is nearly up for your squash, take it out of the oven, scatter the coconut over the top and put back into the oven for a couple of minutes to toast.

Mix the yoghurt with the lime zest and juice and the ground cardamom seeds. Season with a little salt and pepper and mix well.

Take everything out of the oven and scatter over a big platter. Top with a drizzle of the cardamom yoghurt and a little more lime if it's needed.

SERVES 4

1 butternut or other
similar-size squash
olive or coconut oil
seeds from 1 cardamom pod
300g cherry tomatoes
a thumb-size piece of fresh ginger
1 × 400g tin of black beans
50g flaked coconut

TO SERVE
100ml good Greek
or coconut yoghurt
the zest and juice of 1 unwaxed lime
seeds from 1 cardamom pod

10 favourite suppers
from 10 favourite veg

BEETROOT

Beet and kale sauté, serves 2

Take 4 cooked beetroots, roughly slice and sauté in olive oil for 10 minutes, until crisp • Add 2 handfuls of kale and wilt • Top with crumbled walnuts, and, if you like, some goat's cheese.

GREENS

Greens pasta, serves 2

Shred a head of greens and sauté in olive oil with the zest of 1 lemon, 1 chopped red chilli and 1 clove of garlic • When wilted, stir through 150g of cooked pasta • Finish with (vegetarian) Parmesan or pecorino.

BROCCOLI

Broccoli fry, serves 2

Fry 2 large handfuls of purple sprouting broccoli in a little oil with some chilli and soy sauce • Toss with the segments and a little juice from 2 oranges (blood oranges are my favourite) • Serve on top of steamed rice or noodles.

CARROTS

Quick soup, serves 2

Finely chop 4 carrots and sauté with 1 red onion until soft • Add a tin of chopped tomatoes, squeeze in the juice of 1 orange and put in the orange halves • Simmer until the carrots are tender, remove the orange halves then liquidize.

POTATOES

Potato cakes, serves 2

Scrub and grate 250g potatoes and squeeze out moisture • Add dill, 2 eggs, and a scattering of crumbly cheese, such as Lancashire • Form into little cakes. Fry, in a little olive oil, for 4 minutes on each side • Serve with salad and lemon yoghurt.

COURGETTES

Courgette and chickpea stew, serves 2

Finely slice a red onion and sauté in a little olive oil • Add 2 courgettes, sliced into discs the thickness of a £1 coin • Add a handful of halved red cherry tomatoes and cook for 10 minutes • Add a 400g tin of chickpeas, drained • Warm through and serve with bread.

PEPPERS

Spicy roasted red peppers with eggs, serves 2

Take a jar of roasted red peppers and sauté them in olive oil with 1 chopped chilli, 2 chopped tomatoes and a pinch of cumin seeds • Once all soft, break in 2 eggs and bake at 180°C/160°C fan/gas 4 for 12 minutes • Top with chopped parsley.

SWEETCORN

Fresh corn fritters, serves 2

Cut kernels from 2 heads of sweetcorn • Mix with 1 egg, sea salt, black pepper and 1 tablespoon spelt flour • Add chopped red chilli (optional) • Drop heaped tablespoons into a hot frying pan and fry for 2 minutes each side • Top with tomato chutney, leaves and even some slices of halloumi.

PEAS

Quick pea toasts, serves 2

Pod 1kg peas or use 500g frozen peas • Pour over boiling water and drain. Blitz with the juice of ½ a lemon and olive oil • Pile on to toast • Top with goat's cheese or feta, or ribboned courgettes.

SUGAR SNAPS/SPINACH

Green lemon sauté, serves 2

Sauté 2 handfuls of sugar snaps in olive oil with 2 big handfuls of broccoli florets and spinach, ½ clove of garlic and the juice and zest of 1 lemon • Serve with brown rice.

Pan-roast lime feta and chilli greens burrito

This is a dream of a burrito. It's one of those glorious things that manages to balance hearty with fresh, spicy with sharp, smoky with sweet.

I don't like rice in my burrito – to me it's a filler. I'd rather pack it full of flash-fried chilli greens, avocado and smoky lime-spiked beans, but if you are particularly hungry then a scattering of cooked brown rice or quinoa would work here.

Get all your ingredients together. You will need two frying pans, one large and one medium.

Slice the garlic and chilli and put them into a medium frying pan with a little coconut oil. Cook until starting to brown, then add the smoked paprika, the borlotti beans with their liquid and the juice of one lime and let it blip away for 10 minutes to heat through.

Roughly chop the cherry tomatoes and mix them with the juice of half a lime and the chopped coriander. Peel and de-stone the avocados and mash with the juice of the other half lime. De-stem and shred the spring greens. Take the oregano leaves off their stems.

Grate the zest of a lime over the feta or tofu and scatter over a couple of large pinches of chilli flakes. Put 1 teaspoon of coconut oil into a large frying pan and fry the feta or tofu for 3 minutes each side, until just brown, being careful not to move it too much otherwise it will break up.

Once the feta or tofu is browned on both sides, take it out of the pan and cover to keep warm. Add the spring greens and oregano to the same pan, with a little oil if needed, and add the zest of a lime, a good pinch of chilli flakes and 2 tablespoons of water. Cook away the water and sauté until starting to crisp.

MAKES 4 HEALTHY BURRITOS

2 cloves of garlic
1 red chilli
coconut oil
½ teaspoon smoked paprika
1 × 400g tin of borlotti beans
4 unwaxed limes
2 handfuls of cherry tomatoes
a small bunch of fresh coriander
2 ripe avocados
200g spring greens
a few sprigs of fresh oregano
200g feta cheese or firm tofu
red chilli flakes
4 large wholemeal or seeded tortillas

Scoop the beans out of their pan into a serving bowl. When the greens are done, put them into another serving bowl and rinse out and dry the pan. Put it back on a high heat and toast the tortillas in the dry pan. If you have a gas stove you can also do this by holding each tortilla with tongs for a few seconds over the open flame.

Make your own burritos at the table. Lay each tortilla on a plate, leaving a bit of space at the top and bottom. Add the warm beans and top with the greens, a few slices of feta or tofu, a spoonful of the tomato salsa and some mashed avocado. Fold the bottom and top of each tortilla over, then bring the sides in and roll the burrito up. Serve with any extra salsa and avocado.

Grilled avocado barley bowl

This bowl sits at the crossroads of fresh and hearty. It's the kind of food I remember eating when I was growing up in San Francisco. Light, bright and goodness-packed. This dish is a teaming up of all the things that remind me of California: unusual grains, bright citrus, avocado, nuts and seeds, and sprouted seeds and beans.

You can use any grain here – I like pearl barley for its chewy, pillowy heartiness, but quinoa, millet or even brown rice would work a treat. If you are vegan, leave out the feta and use coconut yoghurt. I have used basil, as I usually have a plant sitting on the windowsill, but any soft herb would be good.

This barley salad bowl is just as good the next day and travels particularly well, so I often make it for plane journeys or make extra for lunch the next day.

....

Fill and boil a kettle and get all your ingredients together. Heat a griddle pan on a high heat.

First, get the pearl barley cooking. Rinse it well under cold water, then put it into a pan with twice the amount of water, a good pinch of salt, squeeze in the juice of half a lemon, then put the squeezed lemon half into the pan. Cook for about 25 minutes.

Heat a frying pan on a medium heat. Roughly chop the almonds and toast them in the pan with the seeds until just turning golden brown.

Cut the avocados in half, discard the stones, then put them cut-side down on the griddle pan and cook until they have nice griddle marks.

Make a quick yoghurt sauce: shred the basil leaves and mix with the yoghurt, zest and juice of the remaining lemon and a good pinch of salt and pepper in a small bowl.

SERVES 4

200g pearl barley

the zest and juice of
1½ unwaxed lemons

50g almonds

50g sunflower or pumpkin seeds

2 ripe avocados

a large bunch of fresh basil

200ml plain yoghurt
or coconut yoghurt

100g feta cheese

200g spinach or greens

Grilled avocado barley bowl

Once the barley is cooked, drain any remaining water, then tumble it into a large dish, crumble over the feta cheese and the toasted almonds and seeds. Shred the spinach or greens, add to the dish and mix well. Season with salt and pepper, remembering that the feta is quite salty.

Serve the barley topped with half a warm avocado ready to spoon out, big helpings of yoghurt sauce and more basil, if needed.

Sweet roasted courgettes with crispy chickpeas

This is a very quick and insanely good version of a ratatouille, which was a classic in my house growing up. I use the grill instead of the oven to cook the courgettes quickly and to impart maximum sweet smoky flavour.

I eat this on its own with salad and some quinoa or bread, but if you want to make it a hearty meal you could add some grilled halloumi or baked ricotta (see page 90). Leftovers are amazing in sandwiches or an omelette.

....

Preheat your grill to high and get all your ingredients and equipment together. For this recipe it really speeds things up to have a food processor with a grating attachment. If not, a box grater will do.

Grate the courgettes then scatter evenly on a baking tray, season with salt and pepper, drizzle with a little oil and place under the grill to cook and char for about 20 minutes, turning every couple of minutes.

Meanwhile, put a frying pan on a medium heat. Thinly slice the red onion and add it to the pan with a splash of olive oil and the thyme leaves. Cook for 5 minutes, until soft and sweet.

Finely chop the red peppers and tomatoes and finely slice the garlic. Once the onions are browned, add them to the tray of courgettes with the peppers, tomatoes and garlic and continue to cook and brown, turning every 5 minutes, for a further 10–15 minutes.

Put the frying pan back on a high heat and add a little more olive oil. Add the chickpeas, a good pinch of salt and pepper and the zest of the lemon and cook until the chickpeas are crisped around the edges. This will take about 10 minutes, and you'll need to keep tossing the chickpeas in the pan.

Once the courgette mixture is softened and sweet, and charred in places, scatter over the chickpeas. Serve with some lemon-dressed green leaves.

SERVES 4

4 medium courgettes
olive oil
1 red onion
½ a bunch of fresh thyme
1 × 230g jar of roasted red peppers
550g cherry tomatoes
2 cloves of garlic
1 × 400g tin of chickpeas,
or 250g home-cooked chickpeas
(see pages 241–5)
1 unwaxed lemon

10 simple baked potatoes

SWEET POTATO

Wash and dry 2 sweet potatoes, each weighing 250–300g and prick them with a fork. Roast them at 220°C/200°C fan/gas 7 for 30–45 minutes, until soft throughout. **FOR 2 POTATOES:**

BLITZ 2 tomatoes, 1 chilli, bunch of coriander. **HEAT** black beans, 1 clove of garlic, chilli, pinch of cinnamon. **TOP WITH** beans, chilli sauce, mashed avocado.

SAUTÉ couple of handfuls of spinach. **CHOP** sun-dried tomatoes. **SLICE** avocado. **TOP WITH** hummus, spinach, tomatoes, avocado, lemon juice.

WARM 1 tin of butter beans, pinch of smoked paprika, leaves from a few sprigs of thyme, lemon zest. **CHOP** parsley. **TOP WITH** warm beans, chopped parsley, grating of Manchego.

PAN-FRY 1 tin of drained chickpeas in a little oil, with a teaspoon of cumin, until crisp. **ADD** roasted chopped peppers, cherry tomatoes, parsley, basil, lemon zest. **PILE** on to potatoes and crumble over feta.

HALVE sweet potatoes and scoop out flesh. **MIX WITH** handful of grated Cheddar, sautéed leeks, chopped chives, shredded greens. **PILE** back into skins. **TOP WITH** more cheese. **GRILL** until melted (4–5 minutes). **SERVE** with yoghurt, mixed with lemon juice and chives.

REGULAR POTATO

Wash and dry 2 floury potatoes (Maris Piper or King Edward), weighing about 300–400g, then prick, rub with oil and salt, and bake at 220°C/200°C fan/gas 7 for 1 hour. **FOR 2 POTATOES:**

6

CHOP 6 cornichons, ½ a bunch of parsley, 2 tablespoons capers, zest of 1 lemon. **MIX WITH** 1 tablespoon crème fraîche or Greek yoghurt, salt and pepper. **MASH** into potatoes. **TOP** with rocket.

7

COOK 1 tin of white beans. **ADD** leaves from a sprig of thyme, pinch of chilli, salt. **TOP WITH** beans, grated Cheddar, chilli sauce.

8

CHOP FINELY ½ a cabbage, ½ a bunch of parsley, 1 apple. **GRATE** 1 carrot. **CHOP** 1 red onion, scrunch with juice of ½ a lemon and salt. **MIX** 1 tablespoon yoghurt, juice of ½ a lemon. **PILE** on to potatoes.

9

COOK 1 shredded leek until soft, add greens and wilt, add leaves from 2 sprigs of thyme. **STIR IN** 1 tablespoon wholegrain mustard, 2 tablespoons grated Cheddar. **TOP WITH** leeks and cheese.

10

COOK 1 tablespoon mustard seeds with a handful of curry leaves until they pop. **ADD** handful of spinach and chopped spring onions. **COOK** for 5 minutes. **ADD** zest of a lemon.

Charred mushroom and cashew pizza

My vegan brother Owen regularly puts in requests for things he misses from the old days. Most frequently they're for banoffee pie or a really good pizza, and this is what I make him. I love cooking and eating vegan food – it leaves me feeling light and bright, and I relish how it makes me rethink my cooking because it takes a little more attention.

If vegan cooking can sometimes be considered time-consuming and complicated, or worthy and uninteresting, pizza proves that's not the case. This pizza topping also works amazingly on my cauliflower pizza base from *A Modern Way to Eat*, which is a good gluten-free alternative. I use a little nutritional yeast here to add to the cashews, as it adds depth and is packed with nutrients, but if you can't find it, don't worry, you can just leave it out.

Nutritional yeast is a deactivated yeast that grows on the molasses plant. As its rather matter-of-fact name suggests, it is jam-packed with vitamins, particularly B vitamins including B12, which can be hard to come by in a vegan diet. It's also packed with folic acid, selenium, zinc and protein. But more than anything I like it for its flavour: deeply savoury and umami.

....

First, get all your ingredients together and find yourself a large heavy-based frying pan – you'll need it to be around 26cm. Preheat your grill to maximum.

Slice the red onion and put it into the frying pan with a little oil. Tear the mushrooms into pieces and roughly chop the garlic, then add to the pan with the thyme leaves and cook for 4–5 minutes, turning every so often, until the mushrooms are charred and crispy and cooked through. Remove and put aside for later.

Next, make the cashew ricotta: put all the ingredients into the bowl of a food processor with 3 tablespoons of cold water and blend until completely smooth – this should take 2–5 minutes, depending on how

MAKES 2 LARGE PIZZAS

FOR THE PIZZA
300g light spelt flour
150ml tepid water
1 tablespoon olive oil, plus more for cooking
8 tablespoons good tomato passata
a handful of small black olives, de-stoned
a small handful of rocket

FOR THE MUSHROOMS
1 red onion
olive oil
250g mushrooms
1 clove of garlic
a few sprigs of fresh thyme

FOR THE CASHEW RICOTTA
200g cashews
the juice of ½ an unwaxed lemon
1 clove of garlic
a pinch of fennel seeds
1 tablespoon olive oil
1 tablespoon nutritional yeast (optional)

powerful your machine is. It should be the consistency of normal ricotta. Scoop out into a bowl and wash the processor bowl.

Now make the dough. Put the flour and water into the processor with a good pinch of salt and a tablespoon of olive oil and pulse until the dough comes together in a ball. Tip it out and bring it together in your hands.

Get your frying pan on a medium to high heat. If you have two pans about the right size you can do both the pizzas at once, otherwise you can do one after the other, as they cook quickly. Cut the dough into two equal halves and cover one half for later. Put the other half on to a floured work surface and use a rolling pin to roll it out into a 1cm thick circle about the size of your frying pan.

Drizzle a little oil into the hot pan, then carefully lift in the dough. Leave it on the heat for about 3 minutes, so the base is starting to cook, while you quickly top the pizza.

Spoon half the tomato passata over, then the mushrooms. Dot with the cashew cheese and the olives.

Pop the pizza under the grill for 4–5 minutes, until it is cooked through and the cashew cheese is browned. Repeat with the second pizza.

To finish, strew with some rocket leaves and cut into generous slices. Home-made bliss.

Smoky chowder with maple-toasted coconut

I spent my very first few years living just outside San Francisco. I remember glee-filled trips to the city over the big red bridge – it seemed like a wonderland. These trips were always fuelled by, at my request, Shirley Temples (lemonade and grenadine – a lurid pink glass full of dreams) and deep bowls of chowder, sometimes in hollowed-out sourdough boules, which as a little girl I thought were amazing and very posh.

I still think a good chowder takes a lot of beating for something comforting and nourishing. This is my new version, a warming blanket of a soup, topped with smoky spice and some maple-toasted coconut.

I use some smoked salt here to amp up the smoky flavour. The best stuff, Halen Môn, is made and smoked on Anglesey, where I spend a lot of time and where John is from. If you don't have smoked salt don't worry, your usual sea salt will do just fine.

SERVES 4–6

1 onion
1 stick of celery
coconut or olive oil
2 corn on the cob
1 medium sweet potato
a good pinch of smoked salt
1 tablespoon vegetable stock powder, or ½ a stock cube
½ a large cauliflower
2 limes

FOR THE COCONUT TOPPING
a handful of coconut flakes
1 tablespoon maple syrup
1 teaspoon smoked paprika

TO SERVE
good olive oil
some chopped herbs – parsley, coriander or cresses

Preheat the oven to 200 °C/180 °C fan/gas 6. Fill and boil a kettle and get all your ingredients together. Put a griddle pan on a high heat.

Peel and chop the onion and celery finely and put them into a large saucepan with a tablespoon of oil. Cook for 5 minutes, until soft and sweet.

While this is happening, put the corn on to the hot griddle and char on all sides, turning every minute or so.

Keeping an eye on the corn, peel the sweet potato and chop it into 1cm chunks. Add these to the onion and celery with a good pinch of smoked salt. Pour in 1.25 litres of hot water from the kettle, add the stock powder or cube and bring to a simmer. Roughly chop the cauliflower, add to the soup and simmer until the sweet potato is almost cooked.

Meanwhile, check your corn and keep turning until it is all charred.

Cover a baking tray with greaseproof paper and scatter the coconut flakes on the baking tray with the maple syrup and smoked paprika and toast in the oven until golden; this will take about 4–5 minutes.

Once the corn is charred on all sides, take off the heat and allow to cool before cutting the kernels from the cob – when I do this I rest the corn in a bowl so they don't go everywhere.

Add half the corn to the soup and blitz with a hand-held blender until really creamy and smooth. Squeeze in the juice of the limes, season well, and serve topped with the remaining charred corn, the toasted coconut, some olive oil and herbs or cress.

Sticky green bean and chilli paneer

This is a super-quick but supremely flavourful curry that fills my house with incredible smells. It's spicy, sticky and sweet and, for me, that's the best way to eat paneer. Its roots lie in Kashmir, a place I have never been to but somewhere my parents visited when they were young. They often tell me of its beauty and I imagine it while scooping up this flavour-packed cloud-like paneer.

I show you how to make your own paneer on page 248. It's really simple and is a great vegetarian staple that can be used in most of the dishes where you would use tofu. If you use shop-bought (which I often do), it's best to soak it in a little water for 5 minutes first – this will help it become more cloud-like and it will soak up the flavours better. Kashmiri chilli is available in Indian shops and at good spice shops.

Vegans can make this with firm tofu and it is just as amazing.

....

Get all your ingredients together. If you're using shop-bought paneer, put the paneer in a bowl of water and leave to soak.

Peel and finely chop the onion and garlic. Put the coconut oil into a heavy-bottomed pan and place on a medium heat, then add the onion and garlic and cook for about 5 minutes, until soft and sweet and beginning to brown.

Trim the tops from your green beans.

Add all the dry spices, then turn the heat to low and stir for a little while to toast the spices and release their flavours.

Roughly chop the tomatoes and peel and roughly chop the ginger. Add them to the pan and cook for another 2–3 minutes over a high heat.

Add the green beans to the pan along with the juice of the lemon and the honey and stir to coat them with the spices. Add 100ml of water and cook

SERVES 4

1 medium onion

3 cloves of garlic

2 tablespoons coconut oil

500g green beans

1 tablespoon cumin seeds

1 teaspoon turmeric

1 teaspoon Kashmiri chilli or mild chilli powder

1 heaped teaspoon ground coriander

4 vine tomatoes, or 200g cherry tomatoes

a large thumb-size piece of fresh ginger

1 lemon

1 tablespoon runny honey

1 red chilli

200g paneer

TO SERVE

1 lemon

a small bunch of fresh coriander

a few chapattis or flatbreads

for a couple of minutes, until the beans have lost their rawness, all the water has evaporated and everything is well coated. This will take about 4 minutes.

Finely chop the red chilli. Drain the paneer and roughly cut into 2cm slices. Add them to the pan and stir to coat with all the tomatoes and spices.

Season well with sea salt. Squeeze over the juice of the lemon, then chop the coriander and scatter it over. Serve with warm chapattis or flatbreads for scooping, mango chutney and some rice if you are really hungry (the cauliflower rice on page 88 works well).

Rye pancakes with crispy Jerusalem artichokes

These are deliciously savoury rye pancakes which I top with some flash-fried Jerusalem artichokes, but outside of their short season some new potatoes will do just as well.

If you don't buy rye flour often, do think about trying it here. It makes a rich, filling and super-satisfying bread (see page 254), and it's great in brownies and any chocolate baking.

I often make a double batch of these pancakes and store them in the fridge to use throughout the week for quesadillas and burritos.

....

Get all your ingredients and equipment together. You'll need a large non-stick frying pan.

To make the batter, combine the flours and salt in a bowl. Use a fork to stir in the eggs until the batter is raggedy, then gradually whisk in the water. The batter may seem a bit thin, but it will thicken as it rests for 5 minutes while you get on with the toppings.

Use a mandolin or your excellent knife skills to very finely slice the artichokes or potatoes, there is no need to peel. Finely chop the spring onions.

Heat a tablespoon of olive oil in a large frying pan and add the drained capers. Leave to cook for 4 minutes, until crispy, then scoop out with a slotted spoon and leave to one side.

Leave the pan on the heat and add the artichoke or potato slices. Fry them on a high heat, turning every so often, for about 10 minutes, or until they are starting to crisp and becoming golden. Add the spring onions and fry for a further 3 minutes, then grate over the zest of a lemon and add the juice of half the lemon; place over a low heat while you make the pancakes.

**SERVES 4
(MAKES 8–10 PANCAKES)**

FOR THE PANCAKE
110g rye flour
100g spelt flour
a good pinch of sea salt
3 free-range or organic eggs
500ml water, plus more if needed
olive oil

FOR THE TOPPING
400g Jerusalem artichokes
or new potatoes
4 spring onions
2 tablespoons capers
1 unwaxed lemon
200g ricotta cheese
60g rocket
1 red chilli (optional)

Rye pancakes with crispy
Jerusalem artichokes

Heat a medium frying pan on a medium heat. Rub the pan with a touch
of oil, then pour in just enough batter to thinly coat the bottom. As you
pour, rotate the pan so the batter runs to cover the entire base of the pan.
Cook for a couple of minutes, until the pancake is browned, then flip with
a spatula to brown the second side.

If you are making a few pancakes, put your oven on low, stack them on
a plate as you make them and keep them warm in the oven.

Serve topped with the artichokes or potatoes and crispy capers and crumble
over some ricotta. Scatter over the rocket and finish with a final squeeze
of lemon juice and, if you like, some chopped fresh red chilli.

Winter chopped salad with candied seeds

Two things seem to happen around the same day in late summer. I start wearing socks and I stop eating salads. When I say I stop, I mean I stop being able to find them a satisfying meal, not that I don't let a single piece of rocket pass my lips until the sun comes out again. This salad is the exception. It's pretty much all raw and flavour-packed but it comes with such a feeling of autumn that I relish it even when the woolly hats come out. I use a variety of different-coloured carrots and beetroots to keep things interesting. Search them out if you can – they make this salad incredibly beautiful.

SERVES 4 AS A MAIN DISH, 6 AS PART OF A MEAL

FOR THE SALAD

3 carrots

3 beetroots

1 romaine lettuce or a head of winter greens

1 pear

a handful of pecans

a handful of pumpkin seeds

a splash of maple syrup

50g pecorino cheese (optional)

FOR THE DRESSING

3 tablespoons olive oil

the zest and juice of 1 unwaxed lemon

1 tablespoon tahini

1 tablespoon red wine vinegar

Get all your ingredients together.

Peel, chop and shred all the vegetables and the pear as thinly as you can, making sure to shred the greens or lettuce especially thinly; a mandolin may be useful here, but a sharp knife will do just as well.

Put a sheet of greaseproof paper on a small tray or a plate, then put the nuts into a frying pan. Toast briefly, then add the seeds and toast until they smell toasted and are starting to brown. Add the maple syrup and a pinch of salt and stir, then take off the heat, tip on to the greaseproof and leave to cool.

Mix all the dressing ingredients in a little jug.

Put all the shredded veg into a bowl, season with salt and pepper, pour over the dressing and mix well. Shave over the pecorino, if using, and scatter over the nuts and seeds. Serve with flatbreads, and a crumbling of feta or some torn mozzarella for a main meal.

forty-
minute
feasts

These feasts take a little longer but come together in about forty minutes so are easily achievable on a weekday. They have a few more ingredients than the quicker recipes and the little bit of extra time allows more depth and complexity of flavour to develop. Lemon-scented polpette, a mushroom mezze feast, slow-cooked tomato lentils, Buddha bowls of goodness, rainbow root vegetable tacos, deeply scented pho, home-made chickpea pasta, avocado and chips, sweet potato gnocchi pillows, frying pan pies and throw-it-in-the-oven gratins.

A char-grilled mushroom feast

SERVES 4

FOR THE RICE

200g black or wild rice

3 tablespoons currants

2 tablespoons white wine vinegar

½ a small bunch of fresh dill and/or tarragon

FOR THE MARINATED MUSHROOMS

800g interesting mushrooms: king oyster, portobello, chestnut

2 teaspoons smoked paprika

2 tablespoons maple syrup or runny honey

juice of ½ a lemon

2 tablespoons sumac

a good glug of olive oil

FOR THE TZATZIKI

½ a cucumber

½ teaspoon cumin seeds

½ teaspoon fennel seeds

150ml yoghurt of your choice (I use coconut or good Greek)

juice of ½ a lemon

FOR THE HUMMUS

1 teaspoon coriander seeds

8 tablespoons home-made or good shop-bought hummus

the seeds from ½ a pomegranate

FOR THE OLIVE SALSA

a handful of black olives (I use Kalamata)

a small bunch of fresh coriander

This dish is one of the things I like to cook when people come for dinner. It's an unexpected riot of flavour and colour, with lots of interesting, unique elements that sing when eaten together.

A long time ago a brilliant Italian chef taught me to be brave with the heat when it came to mushrooms: a hot pan, not overcrowded, with generous seasoning. And luckily this way of cooking mushrooms is so well suited to speedy cooking. This is how I like mushrooms best. Charred, dense and smoky all at once. Marinating the mushrooms while the griddle heats up is a quick way to get some extra flavour into them. If you don't have a griddle you can use a large frying pan, or, even better, a barbecue.

....

Fill and boil a kettle and get all your ingredients together. Heat a griddle pan.

Weigh out the rice in a mug or measuring jug, making a note of the level it comes up to, then rinse it in cold water and put it into the pan. Fill the mug to the same level with hot water from the kettle and add to the pan, then repeat so you have double the volume of water to rice. Put a lid on the pan and bring to the boil, then turn down the heat and simmer for 30–35 minutes for black rice and about 20 for wild rice. Soak the currants in the white wine vinegar.

Break or chop any large mushrooms into thick slices, put them into a bowl, then add the marinade ingredients and mix well.

To make the tzatziki, grate the cucumber into a bowl. Toast the cumin and fennel seeds in a dry pan and add them to the cucumber, then stir in the yoghurt, the lemon juice and a good pinch of salt and pepper and set aside.

Once the griddle is smoking, add a layer of mushrooms and grill on all sides until charred, crispy and cooked through. Work in batches rather than overcrowding the griddle, as otherwise they won't cook properly. Keep one eye on the mushrooms, turning them as you need to, while you get on with

another couple of jobs. Keep the first couple of batches warm in a low oven while you cook the rest.

Toast the coriander seeds in the dry pan and bash in a pestle and mortar until you have a rough powder, then add to your hummus with some more salt and freshly ground black pepper if needed. Sprinkle over the pomegranate seeds.

De-stone and chop the olives and the coriander together on a board until you have a rough salsa. Scoop into a bowl, season with salt and pepper, then add a little drizzle of oil and put to one side.

Once the rice is cooked, drain any excess water, then mix in the currants and their soaking liquid along with a good pinch of salt and pepper. Chop the dill and tarragon and mix through the rice.

Once all the mushrooms are cooked, turn off the griddle. Pile the rice on to plates, scatter the mushrooms over and serve with big spoons of the olive salsa, hummus and tzatziki. And, if you like, some flatbreads.

Spinach and lemon polpette

These are lovely, light spinach and nutmeg polpette to serve with spaghetti and a quick tomato sauce. But if you want a lighter meal they are just as good with some quinoa and a shock of green salad.

I use vegetarian-friendly Parmesan here, but if you can't get your hands on that, any vegetarian hard cheese will do the trick. For vegans a spoonful of nutritional yeast will echo the flavour of the Parmesan but you will need to add a few more breadcrumbs or oats.

SERVES 4

FOR THE SPINACH POLPETTE
250g spinach
100g cooked Puy lentils
1 free-range or organic egg
a good grating of fresh nutmeg
50g wholemeal breadcrumbs or oats
50g Parmesan cheese
(I use a vegetarian one)
zest of 1 unwaxed lemon
1 clove of garlic

FOR THE SAUCE
300g spaghetti of your choice
(I use wholemeal)
a handful of almonds
2 cloves of garlic
3 tablespoons of olive oil
1 lemon
a small bunch of fresh basil
350g cherry tomatoes

Preheat the oven to 200°C/180°C fan/gas 6. Fill and boil a kettle and get all your ingredients together.

Wash the spinach and remove any tough stalks. Place a large frying pan on a high heat and, when it's hot, add the spinach and dry-fry until wilted and any water has evaporated.

Drain the lentils well if you are using tinned, then put them into a blender and blitz until they are mushy. Add the egg, nutmeg, breadcrumbs or oats, Parmesan, lemon zest and some salt and pepper. Chop the garlic and add this too. Blitz until combined, then remove from the food processor and fold in the spinach.

Divide the mixture into four. From each quarter make 8 small balls. You should end up with 32 balls, each roughly the size of a £2 coin. Place on a baking tray and put into the oven for 15–20 minutes, until crisp and golden.

To make the sauce, put the almonds, garlic and olive oil in a food processor. Blitz to a coarse texture then add the zest and juice of the lemon, the basil leaves and the cherry tomatoes. Blitz again until you have a rough pesto, then season well with salt and pepper.

When the polpette have had 10 minutes, fill a large pan with boiling water, add salt and once at a rolling boil add the pasta and cook according to the packet instructions (usually about 8 minutes).

Once the pasta is cooked, drain it, reserving some of the cooking liquid. Add the pesto and mix well, adding a little of the reserved pasta water to loosen if needed. Tangle the tomatoey pasta into bowls and top with the spinach polpette and a little more Parmesan, if you like.

Silver Lake sweet potato bake

SERVES 4

4 medium sweet potatoes
2 leeks
olive oil or coconut oil
a few sprigs of fresh sage
a few sprigs of fresh thyme
2 large handfuls of spinach
(about 150g)
freshly grated nutmeg

FOR THE TOPPING
2 slices of good bread,
or 2 handfuls of rolled oats
a handful of pecans (about 50g)
a few more sprigs of fresh thyme
2 tablespoons olive oil or coconut oil
1 tablespoon maple syrup
the zest of 1 unwaxed lemon

FOR THE CASHEW CREAM
100g unsalted cashews
300ml unsweetened almond milk

I wrote almost half this book from my sister's house in Silver Lake, Los Angeles. Smack bang in the middle of my stay was Thanksgiving, and the whole Jones clan were, by chance, together. It's not something we've ever celebrated, but in true Jones spirit we joined in, made a huge spread and ate it with all our LA friends. We ate a mixture of recipes I'd been busy testing and tweaking and a few American classics we wanted an excuse to try out.

Ever since I was little I have been fascinated by the sweet potato casserole that graces the table at Thanksgiving, and how could you blame me? It's a sweet-toothed little girl's dream – whipped-up, sweetened mashed potato topped with burnished marshmallows, disguised as a savoury dish and legitimately eaten with your dinner. Weird and wonderful in equal measure.

This is my version, which is a long way from the original: way less sweet (no marshmallows), but sweet potatoes, herbs and a crunchy pecan topping. I now eat this regularly for my dinner, with a simple, super-lemony green salad to cut through the natural sweetness of the sweet potatoes.

....

Preheat your oven to 220°C/200°C fan/gas 7. Fill and boil a kettle and get all your ingredients and equipment together. You will need a medium ovenproof baking dish, the kind you might use for a family lasagne.

Place a frying pan on a high heat. Put a large saucepan on the heat and fill it with boiling water from the kettle. Add a pinch of salt.

Cut the sweet potatoes into 0.5cm thick slices (there is no need to peel). Halve, wash and finely slice the leeks. Once the water is boiling, add the sweet potatoes, bring to the boil and cook for 10 minutes until soft and cooked through but not falling apart.

Put the chopped leeks into the frying pan with a little oil. Roughly chop the sage leaves and add to the pan with the leaves from the thyme, then fry on a medium heat for about 10 minutes, until soft and sweet.

Meanwhile, make the topping. Put the bread or oats into a food processor and blitz until you have crumbs, then add the pecans and thyme leaves and blitz again until the nuts are about the same size as the breadcrumbs. Add the oil, maple syrup and lemon zest, season well and put to one side.

Blitz the cashews until smooth and then add the almond milk and blitz together until you have a really smooth cream.

Wash the spinach and remove any tough stalks. Once the leeks are sweet, add the spinach and cook for a couple of minutes until it has wilted. Drain the sweet potatoes and tumble them into a baking dish, then spread the leeks and spinach on top. Grate over a little nutmeg, season well with salt and pepper and evenly pour over the cashew cream.

Scatter over the breadcrumb or oat topping and put into the oven to roast for 25 minutes, until golden brown. Serve with a zippy, lemony green salad.

My favourite lentils with roast tomatoes and horseradish

Lentils pair so well with tomatoes, and the shock of fiery horseradish and the crisp savoury crumb make this a firmly British dish. I like to serve this with some simple lemon-and-oil-dressed leaves.

Puy lentils lend themselves amazingly to quick cooking – they don't need soaking, they cook in 30 minutes and they're hearty, delicious and creamy. Adding a tomato and a few cloves of garlic to the pan as the lentils cook imparts great flavour. This way with lentils was taught to me by my old friend and long-time boss Jamie Oliver, but I'm pretty sure it's a classic Italian recipe. You will never want to eat lentils any other way.

If you do have time to soak the lentils overnight, it will make them easier to digest. I always try to remember, but if you've forgotten or don't have time it's not the end of the world. I use jarred grated horseradish here, not the creamed kind or the sauce, and the fresh stuff of course works well too. Make this vegan by using a vegan mayo or cream cheese instead of the cottage cheese.

SERVES 4

FOR THE LENTILS
300g Puy lentils, washed
4 cloves of garlic
1 small tomato
a few sprigs of fresh thyme
2 bay leaves
1 tablespoon vegetable stock powder, or ½ a stock cube
a splash of red wine vinegar

FOR THE TOMATOES
400g baby plum tomatoes or cherry tomatoes
1 unwaxed lemon
olive oil
a couple of handfuls of wholemeal breadcrumbs
a small bunch of fresh thyme
1 clove of garlic

FOR THE HORSERADISH SAUCE
2 teaspoons jarred grated horseradish
100ml cottage cheese

Preheat the oven to 220°C/200°C fan/gas 7. Fill and boil a kettle and get all your ingredients together. You'll need a big pan for your lentils.

Put the lentils into the pan with the unpeeled garlic, whole tomato, a few sprigs of the thyme, the bay leaves and the stock powder or cube. Cover with 1 litre of hot water, place on a medium heat, bring to a simmer, then turn the heat down. Blip away for 25–30 minutes, until the lentils are soft and the water has evaporated. If they are looking too dry, top up with a little more boiling water from the kettle.

Meanwhile, roast the tomatoes. Cut them in half and put them cut side up on a baking tray with some salt, pepper and the zest of the lemon. Drizzle them with a little olive oil and put into the oven to roast for 15 minutes.

Next, on another baking tray, mix the breadcrumbs with the thyme and roughly chopped garlic and drizzle with oil. Season with a little salt and pepper and put to one side.

Mix the horseradish with the cottage cheese or cream cheese and set aside.

Once the tomatoes have had 15 minutes, put the tray of breadcrumbs into the oven and cook both for 5 minutes more.

By now the lentils should be cooked and all the water should have evaporated, so scoop out the tomato and the garlic and put them into a bowl. Once cool enough to handle, pop the garlic cloves out of their skins and use a fork to mash them to a paste with the tomato. Stir this paste back through the lentils. Taste, season with salt and pepper, then dress with a generous glug of olive oil and a splash of red wine vinegar.

Once the tomatoes are sticky and the breadcrumbs are crisp, take everything out of the oven. Serve in deep bowls – a generous ladle of lentils topped with the tomatoes, horseradish sauce and finally a scattering of breadcrumbs.

Curry leaf and smoky celeriac pilaf

Kedgeree has long been our Christmas Day breakfast – the waft of spices and the cheery yellow of the eggs feel celebratory – but we eat it for dinner all year round.

Back in India it was originally a vegetarian dish of lentils and rice; the smoked fish and eggs were only added to suit British tastes. I like the mix of smoke with the spice, so I roast celeriac with smoked salt and stir it through; I use Anglesey's Halen Môn smoked salt, but if you can't find it, normal salt will do. I keep my eggs pretty runny, but if you like them firm, boil them for another minute or two.

To make this vegan, as I do for my brother and sister, leave out the eggs and use oil, not butter. If you can't find curry leaves it will be delicious without them too.

SERVES 6

1 large celeriac
coconut oil, butter or ghee
smoked sea salt, or your
normal sea salt
2 onions
2 cloves of garlic
2 green chillies
2 bay leaves
20 curry leaves (optional)
8 cardamom pods
3 teaspoons coriander seeds
3 teaspoons ground turmeric
400g basmati rice
6 free-range or organic eggs
8 tablespoons Greek yoghurt
the juice of 2 lemons
a bunch of fresh parsley
a bunch of fresh coriander

Preheat the oven to 200°C/180°C fan/gas 6. Get all your ingredients and equipment together. Fill and boil a kettle.

Thickly peel the celeriac, getting rid of any green bits, and cut it into 2cm pieces. Put it on a baking tray with a knob of coconut oil or butter, a hefty pinch of smoked salt and a good grind of black pepper and roast for 30 minutes, until tender.

Peel and finely chop the onions and slice the garlic and chillies. Heat a good knob of coconut oil, butter or ghee in a large, ovenproof pan with a lid. Add the onions, garlic, bay and curry leaves and cook on a low heat for 10 minutes, until soft and sweet. Add the bashed cardamom pods and coriander seeds, the turmeric, chillies and a couple of hearty pinches of smoked salt and stir for another 3–4 minutes on a medium heat until the spices smell great. Take a tablespoonful of the onion mixture out of the pan and put aside for later.

Turn the heat up, add the rice and a little more oil if needed, and stir to coat with the oil and spices. Pour in 1 litre of boiling water from the kettle – you want the water to come about 1cm above the rice, so you may need a little more or a little less. Bring to a simmer. Put the lid on and put the whole lot into the oven for 20–25 minutes.

While the rice is cooking, boil the eggs. I boil my eggs in a pan of boiling water for 6 minutes for runny yolks, but cook a little longer if you like them firmer. Cool the eggs in cold water to stop them cooking, then peel and keep to one side.

Mix the yoghurt with a squeeze of lemon, a pinch of smoked salt and the spoonful of spices and onions you set aside earlier.

Once the celeriac and rice have had their time, take them both out of the oven and stir the celeriac through the fluffy rice along with the chopped herbs and the rest of the lemon juice. Cut the eggs in half and lay them on top, then pop the lid back on to keep everything warm. Serve in the middle of the table, with the yoghurt for spooning over.

Buddha bowls

This is a knockout, a Rocky Balboa of a dish. A heady, peanut-spiked curry topped with a bright carrot pickle, crispy kale and a scattering of toasted seeds.

It is based on a brilliant, nourishing bowl I ate at a very grey Glastonbury Festival. Knee-deep in mud, wet through after hours of biblical rain, I was getting a bit grumpy with hunger and was in need of some proper nourishment. These Buddha bowls came to my rescue. This is the version I make at home, which I love. It will taste best standing in the rain, in a field, after walking in circles for at least an hour.

This all comes together in 45 minutes but you do need to stay on top of a few things at once. This list of ingredients may look long, but I promise this is simple to make. I'll talk you through it. If you want to do this really quickly or are feeling very lazy you could use a massaman curry paste – bigger supermarkets stock a good one. I always take the extra few minutes to make the paste, though. You can also make a double batch of the paste and freeze. If you can't get unsalted peanuts, roasted salted ones will do. I rinse with cold water and drain on kitchen paper so it's not a salt overload.

....

Fill and boil a kettle and get all your ingredients and equipment together. You'll need a small food processor or blender for the paste, a couple of large saucepans and a frying pan.

Keeping the skin on, chop the potatoes into 1–2cm chunks. Put them into a pan, cover with boiling water, add some salt, then bring to the boil and cook until tender – this should take about 5 minutes.

Put your brown rice into another pan with twice its volume of cold water, some salt and a knob of coconut oil and put on a high heat to boil for 20–25 minutes. Keep an eye on the rice while you do your other jobs, making sure it doesn't boil dry.

SERVES 4

FOR THE PASTE
½ teaspoon fennel seeds
½ teaspoon coriander seeds
the seeds from 6 cardamom pods
½ teaspoon black peppercorns
½ teaspoon ground cloves
½ teaspoon ground turmeric
½ teaspoon ground cinnamon
½ teaspoon dried chilli flakes
a thumb-size piece of fresh ginger
1 shallot
1 stalk of lemongrass
a large bunch of fresh coriander
2 cloves of garlic
coconut oil

FOR THE CURRY
500g new potatoes
150g unsalted peanuts
1 × 400g tin of coconut milk
2 tablespoons tamarind paste
1 tablespoon runny honey
sea salt
200g green beans, trimmed
200g firm tofu
2 slices of fresh pineapple

THE REST

150g brown basmati rice

coconut oil

2 medium carrots

1 lime

a squeeze of runny honey

a splash of rice wine vinegar

150g kale

50g mixed toasted seeds
(I use a mixture of poppy,
sesame and pumpkin)

Next, make the paste. Toast the fennel, coriander and cardamom seeds and the peppercorns in a dry pan for a couple of minutes, then put into a food processor with all the other ground spices and the chilli flakes. Peel and roughly chop the ginger and shallot, discard the tough outer layer of the lemongrass and chop the inner stalk, then add it all to the processor. Cut the stalks off the coriander and add these with the garlic. Add a couple of tablespoons of coconut oil and blend on high until you have a paste.

Heat a large pan on a high heat, then add the peanuts and stir for a minute before adding the paste. Fry for a couple of minutes more, then add the coconut milk, tamarind, honey and a good pinch of salt. Drain the potatoes, add them to the sauce and cook for 5–10 minutes until it's a good consistency.

To make the quick pickle, grate the carrots into a bowl and add the zest and juice of a lime, a squeeze of honey, a splash of vinegar and a pinch of salt. Finely chop the coriander leaves and add to the bowl, then put to one side.

Use the pan you toasted the spices in to pan-fry the kale on a medium heat in a little coconut oil, adding some salt and freshly ground black pepper, until wilted but starting to crisp.

Once the potatoes have had 5 minutes in the sauce, add the green beans. Cut the tofu into 1cm lengths, then cut the pineapple into pieces about the same size, discarding the skin. Add both to the curry and simmer for a few minutes, topping up with hot water if the curry is getting dry.

Once the rice and the curry are ready, ladle the rice into bowls and top generously with the curry. Finish off with a pinch of carrot pickle, some greens and a sprinkling of seeds.

Smoky root tacos with green chilli salsa

I like everything about tacos. The way they get scooped up in hands, the way they layer flavour and texture, and the way you can put bowls of each brightly coloured filling in the middle of the table for everyone to help themselves and make their tacos their way.

I make tacos a lot at home, so I have been experimenting with lots of flavours. I wanted a version that was flavour-packed but super quick and easy. So these are a happy marriage of chipotle, crispy root veg, sweet onions, pickled cabbage and a spicy green-chilli-and-coriander-spiked sauce.

I use 100 per cent corn tortillas here – I buy them online in big batches from www.coolchilecompany.com and freeze them until they are needed. You can buy authentic tortillas in some delis and wholefood shops too. If you can't get your hands on them, regular flour tortillas (the smallest ones you can find) stand in nicely.

SERVES 4

3 medium beetroots (about 250g)

2 sweet potatoes (about 500g)

3 tablespoons coconut oil

½ a bunch of spring onions

a small bunch of fresh coriander

2 carrots

a small bunch of radishes

2 unwaxed limes

2 ripe avocados

1 teaspoon chipotle paste, or 1 red chilli

1 teaspoon smoked paprika

a tiny squeeze of runny honey

8 corn tortillas

FOR THE SALSA

2 tomatoes

1 tablespoon chipotle paste

1 green chilli

1 tablespoon maple syrup

1 tablespoon red wine vinegar

Fill and boil the kettle and get all your ingredients together.

Peel the beetroots and, using a sharp knife or a mandolin, slice them as thinly as possible. Chop the sweet potatoes into 2cm chunks. Put the sweet potato into a small saucepan. Cover with boiling water, add a pinch of salt and put on a high heat. Bring to the boil, then simmer for 10 minutes, until soft.

Put a large frying pan on a high heat and add 2 tablespoons of coconut oil. Slice the spring onions as finely as you can, then add to the pan and sauté for 2–3 minutes, until beginning to brown. Remove from the pan and keep to one side. Add the beetroot slices to the pan and fry until crisp. You might need to do this in batches, depending on the size of your pan. Keep a close eye on them as they will brown quickly. Remove from the pan, and drain on some kitchen paper.

Meanwhile, make the salsa. Put all the ingredients into a blender with
a good pinch of salt and the stalks from the bunch of coriander and whiz
until you have a spoonable, pretty smooth salsa. Season well with salt and
pepper and set aside.

Using a vegetable peeler, peel the carrots and radishes into strips, then
put them into a bowl with the juice and zest of a lime, a good pinch of salt
and mix well.

Cut the avocados in half and pop out the stones. Using a knife, slice them
finely all the way to the skin, then use a spoon to scoop out the sliced flesh.

Drain the sweet potatoes and put them back into the pan. Chop the coriander
leaves and add to the pan with the chipotle paste or chopped red chilli,
smoked paprika, honey, cooked spring onions and a good pinch of salt
and pepper.

Warm the tortillas by holding each one over a flame for a few seconds
on each side (if you don't have a gas stove you can warm them in a hot pan).

When you are ready to eat, spread equal amounts of the sweet potatoes over
each taco, top with the carrot and radish, crispy beets, some avocado and
a little of the chilli salsa.

Parsnip rösti supper

There is something clean and Alpine about rösti, at the same time as being super-satisfying. Using parsnips in a rösti adds a sweetness and savouriness that a potato rösti doesn't have.

Here the rösti is served with griddled leeks and lemony greens, with the option to add a little ricotta.

....

Preheat the oven to 220°C/200°C fan/gas 7, and get all your ingredients together. Heat a griddle pan on a high heat.

Beat two eggs together. Peel the parsnips and potatoes and coarsely grate them into a mixing bowl. Squeeze the grated vegetables in your hands or in a clean tea towel to get rid of most of the moisture, then put back into the bowl and add the beaten eggs and the thyme leaves. Season with salt and pepper and mix well.

Heat an ovenproof shallow casserole or frying pan, then add a good drizzle of oil and the parsnip mixture. Pat out to form a thick rösti and cook on a high heat for a couple of minutes, then put into the oven and roast for 20 minutes.

Next griddle the leeks until charred on all sides and then put into the oven to keep warm with the rösti. Wilt the spinach in a frying pan with a little olive oil, then take off the heat and season well with sea salt and black pepper and grate over the zest of the lemon.

A couple of minutes before your rösti is ready, fry the eggs in a little ghee. Once the rösti has had its time, take out the leeks and mix them with the spinach. Pile this on top of the rösti with the ricotta.

SERVES 4–6

FOR THE RÖSTI
2 free-range or organic eggs
600g parsnips (about 4–6)
2 large potatoes
a small bunch of fresh thyme
olive oil

FOR THE TOPPING
150g baby leeks
200g spinach
1 unwaxed lemon

TO SERVE (OPTIONAL)
6 free-range or organic eggs
ghee
100g ricotta cheese

Fragrant herb and star anise pho

I love the idea of pho: noodles, herbs and a soothing broth. But most pho is made with a bone broth. Some places make a vegetarian version, but I have to say I have never had a good one so I've always felt a bit left out of the pho craze. This is a killer vegetarian version. The key here is charring the onions and garlic well first, which gives a rich, smoky flavour to the stock. I have made this for a number of pho connoisseurs and it got the seal of approval.

I often make double the amount of stock in my biggest pan and freeze half to use as a really full-flavoured addition to soups and stews. You can use normal basil here, but if you are lucky enough to be able to get your hands on them you could also use shiso/parilla and Vietnamese mint and basil.

If you are really hungry then some pan-fried tofu, tossed in maple and soy at the end of cooking, would be a good addition.

....

Fill and boil a kettle and get all your ingredients together. Heat a large saucepan over a high heat.

Peel and quarter the onions and halve the bulb of garlic, bash the ginger until it almost starts to break up. Add the onion, ginger and garlic to the dry pan and toast until blackened and charred all over. This will take 4–5 minutes.

Next, add the cinnamon, star anise, cloves and coriander seeds and toast for a couple of minutes, until they smell amazing, stirring all the time. Now add 2 litres of hot water from the kettle, the stock powder or cube, the mushrooms and the soy or tamari and bring to a simmer. Chop the carrots into 2cm chunks and add these too. Cook for 25 minutes, until all the flavours have infused.

While the stock is simmering, fill and boil the kettle. Put the noodles into a bowl, cover with boiling water and put to one side, draining after 8 minutes or following the instructions on the packet.

SERVES 4

FOR THE STOCK

2 onions

1 bulb of garlic

a small hand of ginger

a 5cm cinnamon stick

4 star anise

3 cloves

1 tablespoon coriander seeds

1 teaspoon of vegetable stock powder, or ½ a stock cube

a large handful of dried mushrooms (Asian if you can find them)

1 tablespoon soy sauce or tamari

4 carrots

FOR THE REST

200g dried flat rice noodles or pho noodles

a small bunch of fresh Thai or Vietnamese basil or other herbs

a small bunch of fresh coriander

300g pak choi or spinach

200g sugar snap peas

4–5 limes

200g beansprouts

good chilli oil

Pick the leaves from the stalks of all your herbs, quarter your pak choi and halve your sugar snap peas, lengthways.

Once the stock has had its time, sieve it into a large bowl and pour it back into the pan. Add the juice of 3–4 limes, depending on how juicy they are. Taste and adjust, making sure the lime, soy and spices come through (I usually add another tablespoon of soy here), then add the sugar snaps and pak choi or greens and simmer for a couple of minutes, until the leaves have wilted a little.

Divide the drained noodles between four bowls and ladle over the stock and vegetables. Serve with beansprouts, herbs and the remaining lime cut into wedges, with some chilli oil for everyone to add as they choose.

Mung bean dhal

Mung bean dhal has long been one of my favourite things to eat when I feel in need of some goodness. It is used in the ayurvedic tradition to nourish and calm the body. Mung beans are naturally high in protein, so they are an amazing thing to include in a plant-based diet. You can find mung beans in all big supermarkets, health food shops and Indian shops. They are little green beans – don't confuse them with mung dal, which are split yellow lentils.

Try to soak your mung beans overnight if you can, as they will cook quicker and be easier to digest. This is a great recipe for doubling up, to freeze in portions for days when nourishment needs to be really quick and easy.

Fill and boil a kettle and get all your ingredients together.

Wash and finely shred the leek or chop the onion, finely slice the garlic and roughly chop the ginger. Heat the coconut oil in a pan over a medium heat, add the mustard seeds and cumin seeds and fry until they start to pop, then add the leek or onion, ginger and garlic and cook for about 8–10 minutes, or until soft and sweet.

Add the rinsed and drained mung beans with 1 litre of boiling water from the kettle and the stock powder or cube. Add the turmeric and cinnamon, then bring to a medium simmer.

Roughly chop the tomato and finely chop the chillies (taking the seeds out if they're really hot ones). Finely chop the coriander stalks and add all these to the pan of mung beans, and simmer for 40 minutes.

Once the mung beans are tender, stir well, season well with sea salt and squeeze in the lemon juice. Stir in the coriander leaves and spinach.

I eat this with some coconut yoghurt and a spoonful of mango or coriander chutney (see page 183 for a good quick one).

SERVES 6

1 leek or onion

2 cloves of garlic

a thumb-size piece of fresh ginger

1 tablespoon coconut oil

1 teaspoon mustard seeds

2 teaspoons cumin seeds

500g mung beans (ideally soaked overnight in cold water)

1 tablespoon vegetable stock powder or 1 stock cube

½ teaspoon ground turmeric

1 teaspoon ground cinnamon

1 medium tomato

2 medium hot chillies

a bunch of fresh coriander

1 tablespoon lemon juice, or to taste

1 large handful of spinach per person

5 one-tray dinners

I love any dinner that's made in one tray – less messing around, less washing-up and nothing to do while it all bakes. Here are some of my favourites, but you can freestyle as long as you mix a couple of veg, a bit of liquid (or a vegetable that will release some liquid), a herb and something hearty like beans or torn-up bread. Use a deep, approximately A4-size baking tray here. Each serves 4.

CRISPY RED PEPPER AND CANNELLINI BAKE

- 4 sliced peppers
- 2 handfuls of cherry tomatoes
- a small bunch of thyme
- 400g tin or 250g cooked cannellini beans
- breadcrumbs to top

•

bake for 40 minutes at 220°C/200°C fan/gas 7

HERBED WINTER ROOT GRATIN

- 800g winter roots, chopped
- a bunch of sage, thyme or rosemary
- 2 torn-up slices of bread
- 100ml veg stock
- olive oil
- orange zest

•

bake for 50 minutes at 220°C/200°C fan/gas 7

COURGETTE, LEMON AND
BUTTER BEAN TRAYBAKE

- 4 courgettes, sliced
- 200g spinach
- 400g tin of butter beans
- zest of 1 lemon
- 100ml veg stock
- basil to finish

•

bake for 30 minutes at
220°C/200°C fan/gas 7

SQUASH, PAPRIKA AND
CHICKPEA BAKE

- 1 roughly chopped squash
- 400g tin of chickpeas
- pinch of smoked paprika
- ½ a jar of roasted red peppers
- 100ml veg stock
- 1 chopped red chilli

•

bake for 50 minutes at
220°C/200°C fan/gas 7

TRAY-BAKED SWEET
POTATO RÖSTI

- 600g grated sweet potatoes
- Dijon mustard
- spinach
- peas
- lemon zest

•

bake for 40 minutes at
220°C/200°C fan/gas 7, like a rösti,
top with poached eggs

Celeriac, bay and mushroom ragù

This is my kind of comfort food, unfussy and warming but naturally rich and amazingly tasty. This is deep, wintry, woody food for cold nights under blankets with the fire going. It also makes a brilliant pie or tart filling too.

I eat this with mashed roots or quick polenta, depending on what I've got in the cupboard. I use cider here, as I like its sweet notes alongside the celeriac, but white wine would work just as well.

If I can get my hands on them I use wild mushrooms, but chestnut or some of the more exotic mushrooms from your greengrocer's will be great too.

SERVES 4–6

1 leek
1 red onion
olive oil
1 large carrot
2 sticks of celery
250g mixed mushrooms
4 cloves of garlic
1 medium celeriac (about 800g)
a couple of sprigs of fresh sage
a couple of bay leaves
a few sprigs of fresh thyme
20 black peppercorns
300ml good cider
2 tablespoons vegetarian Worcestershire sauce
1 tablespoon low-salt vegetable stock powder, or ½ a low-salt stock cube

FOR THE HERB OIL
a small bunch of thyme or rosemary
4 tablespoons extra virgin olive oil

TO SERVE
mashed potatoes or polenta
a few tablespoons of crème fraîche (optional)
mustard or horseradish

Fill and boil a kettle and get all your ingredients together. Heat a large casserole pan on a high heat.

Chop the leek and onion and add these to the casserole pan with a glug of olive oil, stirring from time to time while you chop the carrot and celery roughly. Add these to the pan too and cook for 5 minutes, stirring while you get on with some more chopping.

Heat a large frying pan on a high heat. Chop the mushrooms, or tear them into bite-sized pieces, then add to the frying pan with a little olive oil and allow to cook for a couple of minutes. Chop the garlic, and add to the pan when the mushrooms are nearly ready. You want the mushrooms to be starting to brown and crisp around the edges.

Peel and chop the celeriac into roughly 1cm pieces. Once the vegetables in the casserole have had 5 minutes, add the herbs along with the mushrooms and chopped celeriac and cook for a couple of minutes. Add the peppercorns, cider, Worcestershire sauce and stock and bring to the boil, then simmer for 20–30 minutes until you have a thick, rich sauce.

Now get on with whatever you are going to serve this with – I favour polenta or mashed sweet potatoes. But a good potato mash works perfectly too.

To make your herb oil, put all the herbs into a blender with a drizzle of the oil and blitz, adding more oil until you have a grassy green paste.

Once the ragù is ready, spoon it into a bowl on top of a pile of polenta or mash and drizzle over the herb oil. Add a little crème fraîche, mustard or horseradish, if you like. Winter in a bowl.

Frying-pan Turkish flatbreads with spoon salad

The part of east London I live in is full of Turkish cafés. They turn out charcoal-baked flatbreads and insanely good salads, and although meat is front and centre in Turkish food, there are some amazing vegetable dishes too.

Here is a quick way to make my two favourites at home. Amazing, fluffy, quick Turkish flatbreads from the frying pan, topped with caramel onions and smoky red peppers, and my favourite ever salad – sometimes called ezme salad, but I prefer its other name: spoon salad.

I use Turkish chilli here, which has a milder flavour, somewhere between a chilli and a red pepper, but if you can't get your hands on it you can use regular dried chilli flakes, more sparingly. Similarly, if you can't get pomegranate molasses a 50:50 mixture of good balsamic and honey will do.

These flatbreads are brilliantly flavour-packed as they are, but sometimes to mix things up I add some crumbled feta on top. If you are in a hurry, this topping can be used to top ready-made pittas or flatbreads, which will save a lot of time.

....

Get all your ingredients together.

Put all the flatbread ingredients into the bowl of your food processor and pulse until the mixture forms a ball. If you don't have a food processor, this can be done in a bowl using a fork to begin with, followed by your hands, but it will take a little longer.

Dust a clean work surface with flour and tip out the dough. Knead for a minute or so to bring it all together. This is a quick flatbread recipe, so you don't need to knead it for long. Put the dough into a flour-dusted bowl and cover with a plate. Put to one side to rise a little for 10–15 minutes while you do some other jobs. Don't expect it to rise like normal dough, but it may puff up a tiny bit.

SERVES 4

FOR THE FLATBREADS
200g spelt flour, plus extra for dusting
1 teaspoon baking powder
200g Greek yoghurt, or 150ml warm water

FOR THE TOPPING
2 red onions
3 red peppers
2 tablespoons olive oil
1 teaspoon dried Turkish chilli flakes (see introduction)
1 green chilli
a small bunch of fresh mint

FOR THE SALAD
1 red onion
1 lemon
5 ripe vine tomatoes
a small bunch of fresh mint
a small bunch of fresh parsley
1 tablespoon sumac
1 teaspoon harissa or Turkish chilli paste
2 tablespoons pomegranate molasses
extra virgin olive oil

To make the topping, heat a frying pan on a medium heat, then finely chop your onions and red peppers and put them into the pan with 1 tablespoon of oil. Cook on a medium heat for 10 minutes, until soft and sweet, then add the dried chilli. Chop the fresh green chilli and mint and add to the pan along with a final tablespoon of oil. Stir, then take off the heat and season well.

Next, make your salad. Finely slice the onion and put into a bowl with the juice of half a lemon and a good pinch of salt. Scrunch with your hands, then leave to pickle.

Chop the tomatoes roughly, then roughly chop the leaves of the fresh herbs. Put them into a bowl with the spices and the pomegranate molasses and add the lemon-pickled red onions. Season well with salt and pepper and add a little more lemon juice and a good drizzle of olive oil, balancing out the flavours until it tastes great.

Now back to the flatbreads. Put a large frying pan or griddle pan (about 22–24cm) on a medium heat.

Dust a clean work surface and rolling pin with flour, then divide the dough into four equal-sized pieces. Using your hands, pat and flatten out the dough, then use the rolling pin to roll each piece into about a 20cm round, roughly 2–3mm thick.

Once your pan is hot, cook each flatbread for 1–2 minutes on each side, until nicely puffed up, turning with tongs.

Spread with the onion and chilli mixture while hot, and serve straightaway with spoonfuls of salad.

Supper samosas and quick mango pickle

Samosas are always seen as a snack and are often deep-fried and full of what I call school dinners veg: carrots, peas, potatoes. Good as they are that way, these are a little different – fresher, cleaner and oven-baked.

I make them into the main event of my dinner and pair them with a quick home-made mango pickle and a speedy grated carrot salad with some chopped coriander and toasted cumin thrown in. The folding can take a bit of practice. If you get stuck, there are some brilliant videos online that might help you out.

....

Preheat the oven to 220°C/200°C fan/gas 7 and get all your ingredients together.

Blitz the cauliflower in a food processor until you have rice-like shards.

Finely chop the spring onions and put them into a pan with a little coconut oil or ghee. Fry for a couple of minutes, until beginning to brown. Add the chopped chilli and garlic, then the spices and curry leaves and cook for another 2 minutes. Add the cauliflower, spinach, coriander, a squeeze of lemon and a good pinch of salt and cook for 5 minutes, then lay the mixture on a tray to cool down quickly.

Melt the 4 tablespoons of coconut oil or ghee and have this ready along with a pastry brush. Remove your filo pastry from the packet and keep under a damp cloth or tea towel to stop it from drying out.

Lay one sheet of the pastry on a clean, dry work surface and cut it lengthways into three long equal pieces. Put a heaped teaspoon of the cauliflower mixture on the bottom left of the pastry then fold the right hand corner over the mixture, this will create a triangle shape. Continue the folding, keeping the triangle shape, brushing a little oil in between each fold. You should then have a nicely triangular-shaped samosa. Give it a final brush with oil and

SERVES 6
(MAKES 24 SAMOSAS)

400g cauliflower

4 spring onions

4 tablespoons coconut oil or ghee

1 green chilli

2 cloves of garlic

1 teaspoon cumin seeds

1 teaspoon mustard seeds

1 teaspoon garam masala

a small handful of curry leaves

2 big handfuls of spinach

a bunch of fresh coriander

1 lemon

1 × 250–300g filo pastry
(12 sheets)

nigella seeds

FOR THE MANGO PICKLE

2 ripe mangoes

1 teaspoon nigella seeds

a pinch of fennel seeds

a pinch of mustard seeds

1 clove of garlic

the zest and juice of 1 unwaxed lime

1 tablespoon white wine vinegar

sprinkle with the nigella seeds. Repeat with the rest of the pastry and the mixture. Bake in the oven for 15 minutes.

Meanwhile, make a quick mango chutney. With the skin still on, cut off the cheeks of each mango, leaving the stone behind. Carefully slice into the cheek, almost all the way into the skin, in 1cm strips, and then across to make 1cm squares. Push from the skin side to flip the mango into a hedgehog, and use a spoon to scrape off the roughly 1cm pieces of flesh. In a small saucepan, toast the spices then add the mango and lime juice and vinegar. Cook for 5 minutes until the mango has started to break down, then take off the heat.

Serve the samosas with the pickle and a quick salad of grated carrot and coriander.

Roast roots, grapes and lentils

This is a dinner I ate one January day when staying with my sister in Silver Lake. LA is never cold, but it's cold enough to crave something substantial and this is filling and hearty without you having to crawl under a blanket on the sofa. Perfect for cooler nights when the winter cravings for bowls of mash and peas have passed.

I try to get my hands on the little sweet potatoes – they are somehow sweeter and bake whole in their jackets quicker – but if you can't get them, big ones cut into quarters will do just fine.

I use interesting smaller squashes here, like the vivid reddish-orange Red Kuri, the deep green and aptly shaped Acorn and the frilly-when-cut Delicata, which all work well, but a standard butternut will do the trick too.

....

Preheat the oven to 220°C/200°C fan/gas 7. Fill and boil a kettle and get all your ingredients together.

Rub the sweet potatoes with a little olive oil and sprinkle with salt, then place on a baking tray and roast in the oven for 40–45 minutes, until soft.

Cut the squash into 1cm slices and break the cauliflower into small florets. Place them both on another baking tray with a good pinch of salt and pepper and a drizzle of olive oil, toss to coat, and roast for about 40 minutes or so.

Now get on with your lentils. Put them into a pan with the unpeeled garlic, whole tomato and bay leaf. Just cover with vegetable stock, place on a medium heat, bring to a simmer and let them blip away for 20–25 minutes, until the lentils are cooked and the water has evaporated. If they are looking too dry, top up with a little boiling water as needed.

Once the lentils are cooked, take the garlic and tomato out of the pan. Pop the garlic out of their skins, mash with the tomato and a couple of spoonfuls

SERVES 6

FOR THE ROASTED ROOTS
4 little sweet potatoes
olive oil
2 small squashes
or 1 small butternut squash
1 small cauliflower
a large bunch of grapes
a small bunch of fresh sage
a small bunch of fresh thyme
the juice of 1 lemon

FOR THE LENTILS
400g Puy lentils, washed
4 cloves of garlic, unpeeled
1 small tomato
1 bay leaf
1 litre vegetable stock

of the lentils, then stir back into the pan with a couple of spoonfuls of olive oil. The lentils should become nice and creamy.

When there is 10 minutes' cooking time left on the squash and sweet potatoes, put the grapes on a baking tray, breaking them up a little. Scatter over the sage leaves and thyme, drizzle with olive oil and roast for 5–10 minutes, until the grapes are sweet and sticky.

Once the grapes are cooked, take them out of the oven and pour the liquid from the tray into a bowl. Add a good glug of olive oil, the juice of a lemon and some salt and pepper. Tumble all the veg and the grapes on to a platter and dress with the grape dressing, put the lentils into a big bowl, and serve both in the middle of the table.

Charred celeriac steaks
with crispy sweet potato fries

Celeriac is a brute of a vegetable, but beneath its gnarly, knobbly exterior lies sweet creamy white flesh which I adore. Celeriac takes on flavour brilliantly and can stand up to some brave flavours and cooking. Here it's marinated, charred on the griddle and basted with chilli and thyme to create a burnished crust.

Salsa verde always reminds me of my days in the kitchen – it was one of the first things I learnt to make as a chef and it's still one of my favourites. It cuts through the sweet smokiness of the celeriac perfectly.

These sweet potatoes are my favourite way to eat fries. Oven-baked and polenta-coated, they are crispy and perfect. If you can't get hold of polenta, another way to ensure really crisp fries without a lot of oil is to place a cooling rack on top of a baking tray and cook the fries on the rack.

This is also a great thing to do on the barbecue – the chips won't take the high heat, but the celeriac steaks will be all the better for some smoky flames.

....

Preheat the oven to 200°C/180°C fan/gas 6. Fill and boil a kettle and get all your ingredients together.

Carefully cut the sweet potatoes into thin sticks about 1cm thick. Place them on a baking tray, drizzle with the oil, season with salt and pepper and scatter over the polenta. Crush the garlic cloves with the side of a knife, add them to the tray, toss the whole lot together and put into the oven for 25 minutes.

Fill a medium saucepan with hot water from the kettle and bring to the boil. Thickly peel the celeriac, then slice it into 2cm thick steaks and blanch in the boiling water for 5 minutes, until just tender.

Finely chop the red chilli and mix it with the lemon juice, maple syrup, thyme leaves and a pinch of salt and pepper to make a marinade.

SERVES 2

2 sweet potatoes
rapeseed or olive oil
1 tablespoon polenta
3 cloves of garlic
1 celeriac
25g Parmesan cheese
(I use a vegetarian one)

FOR THE MARINADE
1 red chilli
zest and juice of 1 unwaxed lemon
1 tablespoon maple syrup
a few sprigs of fresh thyme

FOR THE SALSA VERDE
3 cornichons
1 tablespoon capers
1 small bunch each of fresh mint, basil and parsley
zest and juice of
½ an unwaxed lemon
2 tablespoons extra virgin olive oil

Once the 5 minutes are up, drain the celeriac and put it into the marinade. Preheat a ridged griddle pan on a high heat. Remember to keep an eye on your sweet potatoes and turn them from time to time so that they brown evenly.

To make the salsa verde, roughly chop the cornichons and capers, then add the herbs and chop everything together. Scoop into a bowl, grate in the lemon zest, squeeze in the juice and add 2 tablespoons of oil and 2 tablespoons of the marinade from the celeriac. Taste and season with salt and pepper.

Place the celeriac on a hot griddle for 2–3 minutes on each side, until charred and cooked through, basting with the remaining marinade every minute or so.

Five minutes before the sweet potatoes are ready, turn the oven up to its maximum temperature. Take the fries out, grate over the Parmesan, then pop back into the oven to crisp up.

Serve the steaks with the fries and a generous spoon of salsa verde, and, if you like, with a shock of green salad.

Quick-pickled roasted roots, polenta and carrot-top pesto

My new favourite thing to cook when people come round for dinner – it's quick and satisfying but it's also elegant, super-delicious and surprising.

I'm going to show you a couple of ways to add flavour and create interesting nuances and layers that might be new to you. First I quickly pickle the vegetables before they are roasted, giving a delicious piquant note, which is balanced by a little honey. To top it off I make a pesto of carrot tops, which taste a bit like parsley but are even more grassy and savoury – they are delicious, and it's so satisfying to know that they have not been binned either by me or by the supermarket. If you can't find carrots with tops, a bunch of parsley will do in their place.

....

Preheat the oven to 220°C/200°C fan/gas 7. Fill and boil a kettle and get all your ingredients together.

First, pickle your vegetables. Using a mandolin or your excellent knife skills, peel and finely slice the carrots (saving the tops for later) and beetroots and put them into a large bowl. Squeeze over the juice of 1½ lemons and add the red wine vinegar and honey. Add a couple of pinches of salt and pepper and put to one side.

Now pour 1.5 litres of boiling water into a large saucepan and bring to a simmer on a medium heat. Slowly pour in the polenta, whisking as you go. Add a good pinch of salt and pepper and continue to whisk as the mixture thickens. Add 3 tablespoons of olive oil and whisk it in, then leave on a very low heat to blip away, whisking again from time to time. It will take about 25 minutes to cook.

While this is happening, spread your pickled vegetables out over two baking trays, drizzle with a little oil and put into the oven to roast for 20 minutes. Reserve the pickling liquor for later.

SERVES 4

4 carrots with tops
(see introduction)

4 beetroots

2 lemons

1 tablespoon red wine vinegar

1 tablespoon runny honey

250g polenta

extra virgin olive oil

a small bunch of fresh sage

a grating of Parmesan
or pecorino cheese (I use
a vegetarian one), optional

Keep an eye on the polenta while you make a quick pesto with the carrot tops. Wash the carrot tops well and pat them dry. Blitz them in a food processor with the juice of the other half of the lemon, 3 tablespoons of olive oil, 3 tablespoons of the pickling liquor and a good pinch of salt and pepper.

Turn the vegetables in the oven – they should be starting to brown – and keep stirring the polenta. Pick the sage leaves from the stalks and toss them in a little olive oil.

Once the veg has had 20 minutes, scatter over the sage leaves and put back into the oven for a further 5 minutes.

The polenta is cooked when you can no longer feel the grain – check by tasting a little, but let it cool down on the spoon first, as it will be hot. Once it is ready, season well with salt and pepper and, if you are using it, grate in the cheese.

Serve the polenta topped with the roasted veg and sage and spoonfuls of the carrot-top pesto.

Lentil ragù agrodolce

This is my version of spaghetti Bolognese. This ragù has a real depth of flavour and the wonderful piquancy that agrodolce cooking is all about. I love this with regular pasta or courgetti (see page 90) or even the chickpea pasta on page 196. I switch between them to suit my mood and the season.

This keeps in the fridge for four days and freezes really well. I freeze it in portion-sized batches for super-quick weeknight dinners. Leftovers are also particularly good on top of a jacket potato or roast sweet potato.

Get all your ingredients together. Fill and boil your kettle.

Peel the carrots and cut them into fine dice, then put them into a heavy pan with the oil. Cook on a medium heat while you peel and finely chop the onion, then add this to the pan and cook for another 10 minutes, or until the onion is soft, sweet and nicely browned.

Add the lentils, then pour in the passata and the vegetable stock with half a tin of hot water from the kettle. Roughly chop the dates and the chilli and add to the pan with the vinegar. Simmer for 25 minutes until you have a thick, rich ragù.

Put a large pan of water on to boil for the pasta and salt it generously. Once the lentils have had 25 minutes, cook the pasta or courgetti and drain, reserving a cup or so of the cooking water.

When the lentil ragù is ready, take off the heat and mash half with a potato masher then return to the heat for a couple of minutes.

Once the sauce is ready, add the drained pasta or courgetti and a cup of pasta water if needed. Serve with Parmesan.

SERVES 4

2 carrots

3 tablespoons olive oil

1 onion

1 × 400g tin of Puy lentils,
or 250g home-cooked lentils
(see pages 241–5)

350ml jar of passata

1 teaspoon vegetable stock
powder, or ½ a stock cube

2 medjool dates, chopped

1 deseeded red chilli

2 tablespoons balsamic vinegar

300g pasta of your choice
(I use pappardelle)

TO SERVE
Parmesan cheese
(I use a vegetarian one)

Chickpea pasta with simple tomato sauce

For years I have been dabbling with different grains and gluten-free flours in pursuit of my Holy Grail: a bowl of satisfying but light pasta with bite and backbone that doesn't leave me needing a two-hour nap.

And I think I've cracked it. These super-simple noodles are made from chickpea flour and use flaxseeds to bind them. They are quick and easy to roll by hand but, if you have the time and inclination, a pasta machine would make them neatly perfect.

They are naturally vegan and gluten-free and are all the more interesting and delicious for it.

If you don't use flaxseed at home already and are worried that the remainder of the bag will lurk untouched at the back of the cupboard, don't be – flaxseed is incredibly good for you and is brilliant added to morning smoothies, porridge, cereals and baking. It's one of the best plant-based sources of alpha-linolenic acid, which converts in the body to the same heart-protective, omega-3 fatty acids found in salmon, sardines and mackerel. It also contains both soluble and insoluble fibre, which helps our intestines. In addition, flaxseed is one of the richest dietary sources of lignans, phytoestrogens thought to protect against cancer of the breast, prostate and colon.

SERVES 4

4 tablespoons ground flaxseed
350g chickpea flour, plus extra for dusting
olive oil

FOR THE SAUCE
2 cloves of garlic
1 × 400g tin of chopped tomatoes
a big bunch of fresh basil

TO SERVE (OPTIONAL)
pecorino or Parmesan cheese
(I use a vegetarian one)

....

Fill and boil a kettle and get all your ingredients and equipment together.

Mix together the flaxseed and 150ml warm water and leave it to sit for a couple of minutes until thickened. Put the flax mixture, chickpea flour and 180ml of cold water into a food processor with 1 tablespoon of olive oil and a good pinch of salt, and blitz until it forms a doughy ball. You can do this easily in a bowl by hand too. Wrap the ball of dough in a clean tea towel or clingfilm and set aside for 10 minutes.

Heat a frying pan on a high heat, then thinly slice the garlic and add it to the pan with a little olive oil. Fry for a minute or two, until the edges are beginning to brown. Quickly add the tinned tomatoes and leave to simmer on a medium heat for 10 minutes, until thickened and glossy. Fill a large pan with hot water from the kettle, add a good pinch of salt and bring to the boil, ready for the pasta.

Unwrap your dough and cut it into two pieces. Flour your work surface generously with chickpea flour. Use a rolling pin to roll out the dough as thinly as you can, as it will expand a little as it cooks, then use a knife to cut the dough into 0.5cm ribbons. Place on a floured tray and repeat with the other half of the dough.

Once you have cut all your pasta, add it to the boiling water for 2–3 minutes – no longer or it will start to break up a bit. Don't worry if some of the pasta breaks a little, this pasta is more delicate than the regular sort. Using a slotted spoon, drain it and add it to the tomato sauce with most of the basil leaves. Toss gently to coat all the pasta, adding a little of the cooking water from the pan if it looks a bit thick.

Serve with a little more basil scattered over and some pecorino or Parmesan, if you like.

Beetroot and radicchio gratin

This is a tray of crisp-edged beetroots, winter herbs and golden potatoes. A plate of incredible tones of deep pink and purple – lurid colours, but soft, sweet, warming and super-tasty flavours. The beetroots perfectly counter the gentle bitterness of the radicchio, so if you are new to bitter leaves this is a great place to start. If you can't find radicchio, a couple of red chicory will work well.

Bitter leaves are really good for digestion. They are even thought to help counter cravings for sweet foods, and if you are anything like me, sometimes a bit of help with the sugar cravings can be a good thing.

I top this gratin with a punchy gremolata, chopped fresh herbs with proud amounts of citrus and garlic; the grassy freshness, zippy orange and punch of garlic take this gratin to the next level. I serve it with a watercress salad, but if you like you could have some bread on the side for mopping up the juices.

SERVES 4

750g beetroots
300g small to medium waxy potatoes
1 head of radicchio
a few sprigs of fresh thyme
a few sprigs of fresh sage
3 cloves of garlic
1 unwaxed lemon
125ml white wine
125ml hot vegetable stock

FOR THE GREMOLATA
a small bunch of fresh parsley
½ a clove of garlic
1 red chilli
the zest of 1 large unwaxed orange

Preheat the oven to 220°C/200°C fan/gas 7. Fill and boil a kettle and get all your ingredients and equipment together.

Peel the beetroots and use a food processor or a mandolin to finely slice them. Scatter them in a deep baking dish approximately 20cm × 25cm. Slice the potatoes in the same way and scatter them over the beetroots. Shred the radicchio as you would a lettuce – avoiding and discarding the root – and add this to the tray too.

Pick the leaves off the stalks of the thyme and sage, slice the garlic and add to the dish, then grate over the zest of the lemon and season well with salt and pepper. Toss everything together, then use your hands to press and push everything level in the dish. Pour over the white wine and the hot stock – the liquid should come about halfway up the potatoes – and bake in the oven for 30 minutes.

Meanwhile, make the gremolata. Finely chop the parsley, garlic and chilli and put into a bowl with the orange zest. Mix well, season with a little salt and pepper and put to one side.

Once the gratin is browned on top and crisp around the edges, it should be ready; check by pulling a potato from the middle of the gratin and making sure it's cooked through. Serve with a watercress or rocket salad and, if you like, some bread for mopping up the juices.

quick flavour boosts

HERB OIL

On top of soups,
stews, dressings,
grains, salads,
flatbreads, tofu

A bunch of soft herbs

or

½ a bunch of hardy herbs

+

100ml extra virgin olive oil

+

Sea salt

+

Lemon juice to taste

↓

Blitz until you have a herby
green paste

PESTO

On top of pasta, crostini, pizza,
green veg, baked potatoes,
new potatoes, soups,
sandwiches, tomatoes

A bunch of soft herbs

+

A small handful of nuts

+

½ a clove of garlic
(optional)

+

Sea salt

↓

Bash in pestle and
mortar or blitz

+

2 tablespoons olive oil

+

Juice of 1 lemon

↓

Season and mix well

HERB SMASH

On top of soups,
stews, flatbreads,
bruschetta, stirred through
veg, roasted roots

A bunch of soft herbs

+

Zest of 1 lemon,
orange or lime

+

½ a clove of garlic

+

1 red or green chilli

+

Sea salt and black pepper

↓

Chop all this together
until you have a rough
herb smash

Cooking fast is all about adding and layering flavour, quickly and cleverly. One of the ways to do this at home is to add an instant boost with a simple but flavour-packed dressing or herb oil. These boosters will take a couple of minutes to make and transform a simple bowl of quinoa or a pan of steamed broccoli into a dinner to be proud of. These rough recipes make enough for a few bowls of grains or veg. I have left them quite casual so that you can adapt to your mood and to what they'll be piled on top of.

MISO AND MAPLE DRESSING

On top of noodles, rice, roast veg, green veg, tomatoes, sandwiches

1 tablespoon dark miso

+

1 tablespoon soy sauce

+

1 tablespoon maple syrup

+

1 tablespoon rice vinegar

or

lime juice

↓

Mix well

TAHINI DRESSING

On top of soups, stews, sandwiches, flatbreads, falafels, salads

2 tablespoons tahini

+

Juice and zest of 1 lemon

+

2 tablespoons olive oil

+

1 finely chopped shallot

or

½ a finely grated clove of garlic

+

Sea salt and black pepper

↓

Mix well

HARISSA DRESSING

On top of halloumi, hummus, flatbreads, salads, cheese, soups

Fry 6 chopped spring onions until soft and sweet

+

1 tablespoon harissa

+

2 tablespoons olive oil

+

Juice of 1 lemon

+

Sea salt and black pepper

↓

Mix well

Avocado and chips

This is my new comfort dish. To me it has the homely childhood associations but the flavours are much more sophisticated. If you haven't cooked avocado before, I understand your trepidation – I was sceptical at first too, but it is a revelation. Baking the avocado enhances its butteriness and its grassy-fresh character. I serve this with an amazing home-made instant ketchup and some simple, mashed minty peas.

Use just-ripe avocados here, as the super-ripe ones won't work. This can be made easily with oats in place of breadcrumbs if you prefer. I use a cooling rack and a little polenta to allow the chips to get really crispy in the oven; using a cooling rack means the air circulates all around the chips, helping them crisp up. If you don't have one that fits in your oven that's okay, the chips might take a little longer to crisp.

....

Preheat the oven to 220°C/200°C fan/gas 7. Fill and boil a kettle and get all your ingredients together.

First, chop the courgettes into thin, chip-like batons, avoiding the fluffy middle bits. Pop them on to a baking tray and scatter over the polenta. Grate over the Parmesan, if using, then sprinkle with salt and pepper and toss on the tray to make sure each chip is coated well. Transfer the chips to a cooling rack that fits on top of the baking tray and bake for 35 minutes.

Cut your avocados in half and remove the stones, then carefully scoop out the flesh or peel off the skin, keeping the halves intact.

Mix the breadcrumbs or oats (if they are very big oats, you might want to pulse them in a food processor first) with the chilli, sesame seeds and a good pinch of salt and pepper and put on a plate. Crack the eggs into a deep plate or shallow bowl. Season and whisk with a fork.

SERVES 4

FOR THE CHIPS
4 large courgettes
2 tablespoons polenta
25g Parmesan cheese (I use a vegetarian one), optional

FOR THE AVOCADO
2 just-ripe avocados
100g breadcrumbs or fine oats
a pinch of dried chilli flakes
sesame seeds
2 free-range or organic eggs

FOR THE QUICK TOMATO KETCHUP
1 tablespoon tomato purée
6 cherry tomatoes
a swig of vegetarian Worcestershire sauce
a swig of Tabasco sauce
a dash of maple syrup

FOR THE PEAS
200g frozen peas
a few sprigs of fresh mint

Take the avocado pieces and lower them into the egg mixture, turning them carefully to coat. Then toss in the breadcrumbs so they are coated evenly. Put the avocados into the oven next to the chips and bake for 25 minutes.

Put the peas into a small pan and cover with boiling water. Boil for a couple of minutes while you finely chop the mint. Drain the peas, add the mint and a good pinch of salt and pepper, and mash them a little to smash them up.

Meanwhile, check your avocado and chips, turning them carefully so they cook evenly.

Next, put all the ingredients for the ketchup into a jug and blitz with a hand-held blender until smooth. Season with salt and pepper, then taste and adjust, adding more sweetness or vinegar if needed.

Once the avocado is browned and the chips are crisp, take them out of the oven and serve with the warm, minty peas and generous spoonfuls of ketchup.

Sweet potato and ricotta gnocchi with almond pesto

These gnocchi are my kind of comfort food – light but hearty little sweet potato and ricotta dumplings, tossed in a quick, sweet basil and oregano pesto. Hearty enough for a winter dinner in front of the fire but fresh enough in flavour for an incredible summer supper.

This recipe goes against the gnocchi rules I learnt as a chef. We used to make gnocchi with almost no flour and super-dry baked potatoes; it was delicious but took some skill and a great deal of patience.

This is a foolproof gnocchi recipe that comes together in a life-friendly time. The addition of some flour means the gnocchi are much easier to handle if you haven't made them before, and they are still utterly delicious.

If you are vegan, leave out the ricotta and use 200g more of sweet potatoes. The recipe can easily be made with a gluten-free flour, such as buckwheat flour, as in this case the slightly drying nature of gluten-free flours is a plus.

Any leftover, uncooked gnocchi will keep well in the fridge for 2–3 days.

SERVES 6–8

800g sweet potatoes
200g ricotta cheese
300g light spelt flour
1 free-range or organic egg yolk
a little butter
olive oil

FOR THE PESTO
2 large bunches of fresh basil
a small bunch of fresh oregano
50g blanched almonds
1 unwaxed lemon
extra virgin olive oil
a good grating of pecorino
or Parmesan cheese (I use
a vegetarian one), optional

Fill and boil the kettle and get all your ingredients together.

Peel the sweet potatoes, cut them into large 3cm pieces and steam them; this will take about 20 minutes.

Meanwhile, make your pesto: put the herbs and nuts into a food processor with the zest and juice of the lemon and blitz until you have a grassy green paste, then add olive oil gradually until you have a spoonable pesto. If you want to loosen it without adding too much oil you could add a tablespoon of water. Season well with salt and pepper.

Put a large pan of boiling salted water on a high heat. Drain the sweet potatoes, allow them to steam dry for a couple of minutes to get rid of as

much moisture as possible, then mash them well with a potato masher or a potato ricer.

Fold in the ricotta, flour and the beaten egg yolk. Leave the mixture for 5 minutes, then, on a well-floured surface working with a quarter of the dough at a time, roll it into two long, fattish sausages about 2cm in diameter. Leave for a further couple of minutes to firm up.

Cut the sausages into short 2cm pieces. Keep these to one side while you roll and cut the rest of the gnocchi. Drop them into the boiling water and cook until they rise to the top.

Meanwhile, warm four bowls. Once the gnocchi have risen to the surface, scoop them out of the pan into a big bowl, then stir through the pesto before dividing between the four bowls with an extra grating of Parmesan or pecorino, if you like.

Frying pan squash and cavolo nero pie

This tart is a meeting of two amazing dinners I ate in the same week. One was a light, crisp feta and spinach spanakopita pie in a no-frills Greek café, not far from home. The other was in a great pizza place a few minutes' walk from my house, where I ate a pizza topped with smashed squash, crispy cavolo nero and black olives. I loved the flavours of the pizza so much I wanted to work them into something that was quick enough to make on a weeknight, and this is it.

This is a cheat's pie that uses a frying pan instead of a tart tin and is filled with super-quick grated and shredded veg.

Preheat your oven to 220°C/200°C fan/gas 7 and get all your ingredients together. You'll need a 24cm frying pan.

Heat a saucepan on a low heat while you finely chop your onions, then turn the heat up to medium, add a little coconut oil and cook the onions for 5 minutes, until soft and sweet.

While the onions are cooking, peel and roughly dice the squash. Add it to the onions along with the thyme leaves and cook for 5–10 minutes, until the mixture is dry.

Meanwhile, unwrap the sheets of filo and lay them over your frying pan, leaving a little overlap round the edges (you'll fold this in later). Keep laying the filo in the pan until you have a good sturdy 3–4 sheet layer all over – you may need to patch it together bit by bit if you have small sheets.

Once the squash has had 5 minutes, scoop it into a bowl. Crack in the eggs and grate in the pecorino or Parmesan. Season with freshly ground black pepper and mix well.

SERVES 4–6

2 red onions
coconut or olive oil
450g butternut squash
½ a bunch of fresh thyme
1 × 200g pack of filo pastry
2 free-range or organic eggs
100g pecorino or Parmesan cheese (I use a vegetarian one)
olive oil
200g cavolo nero or kale
1 unwaxed lemon
100g goat's cheese
100g black olives (I use Kalamata)

Drizzle the filo pastry with a little olive oil, then use a pastry brush to persuade the oil all over the pastry. Spoon the butternut mixture into the pan and put on a medium heat.

Working quickly, shred the cavolo nero and toss it with the juice and zest of the lemon and a little oil. Scatter it on top of the butternut and push down a little into the mixture, then dot the goat's cheese and de-stoned olives on top. Fold the excess filo back over the filling to form a wavy edge. Place on the bottom of the oven and bake for 20–25 minutes, or until golden and crisp.

Take out, cut into six generous slices and serve with a lemon-dressed green salad and, if you like, some chilli sauce.

Butternut and cannellini gratin

This is a favourite warming winter or autumn dinner. It's crispy-topped, with a sweet butternut, lemon and herb filling. It's super-easy to put together and is made from simple stuff that I usually have to hand.

Try experimenting with other squashes if you find them in the greengrocer's, as they all cook in roughly the same amount of time. Mixing a few different colours and shapes can be really pretty and make it more interesting to eat.

If you are vegan, or if you just fancy changing this up, you can add a handful of chopped almonds in place of the cheese; it's not the same, but it's just as good.

....

Preheat your oven to 220°C/200°C fan/gas 7 and get all your ingredients and equipment together.

Roughly slice the onions. Put a wide, shallow ovenproof saucepan on a medium heat, add a good glug of olive oil and fry the onions until soft and sweet.

Cut the squash into large dice, discarding the seeds (there is no need to peel), then add to the softened onions with the leaves from the rosemary sprigs and continue cooking until the squash has coloured a little at the edges and is starting to soften; this will take about 10 minutes.

Take off the heat and add the drained cannellini beans, then season with salt and black pepper, squeeze over the juice of the lemon.

Pour over the stock, then tear the bread over the top. Grate over the Gruyère or sprinkle over the chopped almonds, if you like. Bake for 35–45 minutes, until the cheese has melted and the stock is bubbling around the edges.

SERVES 6

3 red onions

olive oil

1kg butternut or other orange-fleshed squash

a few sprigs of fresh rosemary

2 × 400g tins of cannellini beans, or 500g home-cooked beans (see pages 241–5)

1 lemon

300ml hot vegetable stock

3 thick slices of good sourdough or wholemeal bread

150g Gruyère cheese (see introduction if you're vegan)

Roasted coconut, lime and tamarind curry

This recipe, like the sweet potato dhal in *A Modern Way to Eat*, has become an instant classic in my house. I make this a lot, and each time I make it I still can't believe how tasty it is. The squash, fennel seeds and tamarind come together to make a vibrant curry, and the toasted maple and lime coconut is the crowning glory (and a great little treat for snacking on in its own right too).

If you are in a real rush you could use pre-cooked brown rice here. I usually keep some leftover rice in the freezer (see page 246 on cooking and storing grains), but if you search out one without any additives, the pre-cooked pouches can be a speedy solution if you are in a fix.

SERVES 4

300g short-grain brown rice

1 red onion

coconut oil

2 cloves of garlic

a thumb-sized piece of fresh ginger

1 red chilli

2 carrots

a large bunch of fresh coriander

400g butternut, kabocha or acorn squash

1 × 200g bag of spinach or other greens

1 tablespoon fennel seeds

1 tablespoon mustard seeds

1 × 400g tin of good chopped tomatoes

1 × 400g tin of coconut milk

2 tablespoons tamarind paste

500g unsweetened coconut flakes or desiccated coconut

2 unwaxed limes

2 tablespoons maple syrup

Preheat your oven to 200°C/180°C fan/gas 6. Fill and boil a kettle and get all your ingredients together. Put a big saucepan on a medium heat.

Get your rice on. Weigh out the rice in a mug or measuring jug, making a note of the level it comes up to, then rinse it in cold water and put it into the pan. Fill the mug to the same level with water and add to the pan, then repeat so you have double the volume of water to rice. Add a good pinch of salt, bring to the boil, then turn down the heat and simmer for 20 minutes.

Meanwhile, peel and finely chop the red onion. Put a teaspoon of coconut oil into another large saucepan, add the onion and cook on a high heat for 5 minutes, until soft.

Chop the garlic, ginger and chilli and put to one side. Peel the carrots and chop into 0.5cm rounds. Chop the coriander stalks, put the leaves to one side. Once the onion is soft, add the garlic, ginger, chilli, carrots and coriander stalks to the pan and cook for a couple of minutes.

Cut the squash in half lengthways (there is no need to peel) and then into quarters. Remove the seeds, then cut into thin 0.5cm slices. Wash the spinach and remove any tough stalks.

Add the fennel and mustard seeds to the pan and allow to cook until the mustard seeds start popping, then add the squash, chopped tomatoes, coconut milk and tamarind paste. Put a lid on the pan and simmer on a medium-high heat for 20 minutes, until you have a thick, flavoursome curry. Top up with a little hot water from the kettle if it gets too thick.

Meanwhile, line a baking tray with greaseproof paper. Put the coconut flakes on the tray and grate over the zest of 1 lime. Pour over the maple syrup and put into the oven for 5 minutes, until turning golden at the edges.

When the rice is ready, drain it and keep it warm. Once the curry is cooked, stir in the spinach and the coriander leaves and squeeze in the juice of both the limes. Spoon some rice into your bowls and ladle the curry over the top. Scatter the roasted coconut on top and finish with more coriander, if you like.

A modern moussaka

I ate this in LA and I have dreamed of it ever since. It's rich, creamy and tasty at the same time as feeling bright and clean.

Be sure to cook your aubergines through on the griddle, as there are few things worse than raw aubergines. They'll be translucent and soft all the way through when they're ready.

I have kept this dish naturally vegan and dairy free, as I find it lighter and more delicious. You could easily swap the coconut oil for butter and almond milk for cow's, to make a more classic béchamel.

....

Preheat the oven to 220°C/200°C fan/gas 7 and heat a griddle pan on high. Fill and boil a kettle and get your ingredients and equipment together.

Halve the tomatoes and finely slice the onions; on a large baking tray, toss them with a drizzle of olive oil, scatter over the chilli, grate over the zest of the lemon and add a little salt and pepper. Put them into the oven to roast for 20 minutes.

Cook the potatoes in boiling water from the kettle for 12–15 minutes, until tender and cooked through.

Meanwhile, slice the aubergines into 0.5cm rounds. Put them on to the hot griddle pan until cooked through and charred on both sides – you will need to do this in batches. Put each cooked batch on a plate, drizzle with a little olive oil and season with salt and pepper.

Make the béchamel: melt the coconut oil in a saucepan, add the flour and cook for a couple of minutes to cook out the rawness, then add the almond milk bit by bit, whisking as you go to make sure there are no lumps. It should be a pretty thick béchamel, similar to Greek yoghurt.

SERVES 4–6

500g cherry tomatoes
2 red onions
olive oil
a pinch of dried chilli flakes
1 lemon
600g small new potatoes
2 aubergines
3 tablespoons coconut oil
3 tablespoons spelt flour
300ml unsweetened almond milk

Once cooked, drain the potatoes. Put a large shallow, heavy-based ovenproof pan on the heat and add 3 tablespoons olive oil, then add the potatoes and use a potato masher to squash them a tiny bit so they have a flat side underneath; leave them to brown a little. Toss every now and then so they are crisp but not sticking to the pan. Season well.

Once the bottoms of the potatoes are brown, take the tomatoes out of the oven and spoon over the potatoes. Top with the griddled aubergine, spoon the béchamel over. Put into the oven to brown under a hot grill for 5–10 minutes.

Once browned and bubbling, serve in the middle of the table with some bright, lemon-dressed leaves.

Crispy chickpea and harissa burger

These burgers are easy to fall for: super simple to put together, highly spiced and with a back-note of sweetness from the dates. I make a double batch and freeze half for quick dinners throughout the week.

Don't be tempted to skip the pickle, it really makes these burgers sing. If you can't get pomegranate molasses or it's a step too far for you, a tablespoon of honey mixed with a tablespoon of punchy balsamic vinegar will stand in for it.

SERVES 6

FOR THE BURGERS
200g cooked quinoa
(100g uncooked)
200g frozen peas
1 × 400g tin of chickpeas or
250g home-cooked chickpeas
(see pages 241–5)
1 teaspoon ground cumin
1 teaspoon ground coriander
½ teaspoon smoked paprika
4 medjool dates
a large bunch of fresh parsley
1 tablespoon harissa
1 tablespoon Dijon mustard
olive or coconut oil
50g sesame seeds

FOR THE RELISH
1 red onion
200g cherry tomatoes
a good drizzle of
pomegranate molasses
a bunch of fresh coriander

TO SERVE
6 good burger buns
hummus
salad leaves

Fill and boil a kettle and get all your ingredients together.

If you need to cook your quinoa, start by toasting it in a pan until you can hear it pop, as this gives it more flavour. Then put it into a mug or measuring jug, making a note of the level it comes up to, and pour it into a large pan. Fill the mug to the same level with boiling water and add to the pan, then repeat so you have double the volume of water to quinoa. Cook until all the water has been absorbed and the little curly grain has been released.

Put the frozen peas into a heatproof bowl, cover them with boiling water and leave them to sit for 10 minutes.

Put the drained chickpeas into a frying pan with the ground cumin, coriander and smoked paprika and toast until all the moisture has gone and they are starting to pop.

Drain the peas very well and put them back into the dry bowl. Tip in half the chickpeas and half the cooked quinoa, then add the dates, parsley, harissa and mustard and use a hand-held blender to blitz until everything is combined. Stir in the rest of the chickpeas and quinoa and mix well.

Divide the mixture into six and shape each one into a burger. Pop them into the fridge to firm up.

To make the relish, finely slice the onion and fry for 8–10 minutes, until soft and sweet. Add the chopped tomatoes and cook for another 5 minutes, until they have broken down, then add the pomegranate molasses. Take off the heat and transfer to a bowl, then roughly chop the coriander and mix in.

While the relish is cooking you can get on with cooking your burgers. Heat a frying pan on a medium heat (you can cook them in batches or have two pans on the go if you prefer). Add a little olive or coconut oil and fry the burgers on each side for 5 minutes, until crisp and warmed through. Once they are done, sprinkle both sides with sesame seeds and cook for another minute on each side to toast. You can also roast the burgers on an oiled tray at 220°C/200°C fan/gas 7 for 20–25 minutes.

Warm the buns in a dry pan and layer the burgers with the hummus, some tomato relish and the salad.

Honey and white miso aubergines

Aubergines and mushrooms fall into the same territory for me: unless they are cooked perfectly I am not interested. So I am very selective with the aubergine recipes that make it to my kitchen, let alone to this book. This one is knockout. Everything an aubergine should be, soft and buttery on the inside, and burnished and just crisp on the outside. The miso paste that is generously spread on top is a fanfare of flavour. I serve this with brown sushi rice, which I buy in a Japanese supermarket or online. It can be hard to come by – white sushi rice will work at a pinch.

Get all your ingredients together and preheat the grill to medium.

First, cook the sushi rice. This is how I like to do it: wash the sushi rice three or four times in cold water, until the water runs clear, then add 400ml of cold water and bring to the boil. Put a lid on and boil for 10–15 minutes for white rice and 15–20 minutes for brown, then turn the heat off and leave the lid on. Don't peek, as it will release the steam, which you need to finish the cooking.

Cut the aubergines in half lengthways, then cut the flesh in a crisscross pattern without cutting into the skin. Brush both sides of each aubergine with the oil. Place on a baking tray cut side down and grill for 5 minutes, then turn them over and grill for a further 5 minutes, until soft all the way through. Turn the oven to 220°C/200°C fan/gas 7 and turn off the grill. Mix the white and dark miso in a bowl with the honey, mirin, chilli powder and a tablespoon of hot water. Rub the cut side of the aubergines with the miso mixture and put back into the oven to cook for 15 minutes.

Heat a pan with a little coconut oil and sauté the kale and pak choi until just cooked, then toss with the soy and the yuzu or lime juice. Take the aubergines out of the oven and sprinkle with the sesame seeds. Take the lid off the rice and stir in the brown rice vinegar. Serve the rice topped with the greens, aubergines and the sticky sauce from the tray spooned over. Top with more sesame seeds if you like.

SERVES 4–6

300g brown sushi rice

4 long, slim aubergines

1 tablespoon melted coconut oil, plus a little extra

2 tablespoons white miso paste

2 tablespoons dark miso paste

2 tablespoons runny honey

2 tablespoons mirin

a heathy pinch of chilli powder

1 head of kale (about 200g)

4 pak choi

a splash of soy sauce or tamari

1 tablespoon yuzu lime or the juice of 1 lime

4 tablespoons toasted black and white sesame seeds

2 tablespoons brown rice or rice wine vinegar

investment
cooking

This kind of cooking is the backbone of my kitchen – smart cooking which means I have some nourishing, delicious food to help me through the week. You don't have to do this every week but, when you have an hour or so to spare, this kind of cooking can soothe your soul and help you put quick suppers together during the week. Not to mention a few treats. Nut butters and tahini, sweet treats, quick granolas, the best banana bread you'll ever taste, miraculous chickpea tofu from scratch, vats of grains and pulses, stocks, soups, my favourite rye bread and home-made coconut yoghurt.

Heavenly nut butters

There is so much joy in making something at home that you usually buy, an unparalleled feeling of smugness. My favourite thing about making cupboard staples at home, though, is the freedom to make things that are truly original, to mix flavours you can't find anywhere else, and tweak and blend things just to my taste.

That is exactly what has happened here. I am in love with nut butter. I eat it on toast or rice cakes for a quick snack, dip fruit in it, use it in dressings and spoon it on to my morning porridge. I often make simple almond butter with a pinch of salt, which is a staple ingredient. These butters are a lot more special, though; they use stellar combinations of flavours at the same time as being raw and nutrient-packed, so you can be sure that you are boosting the flavour and goodness of your meals every time you open a jar.

I've included three different flavoured nut butters here. Coconut and Cardamom Almond Butter is a particular favourite of mine. I find it hard to leave the jar alone. If lucuma is hard to find, or one step too far, you can leave it out. The Salted Date Caramel Pecan Butter is a salted caramel that is acceptable to eat for breakfast and the Hazelnut and Cacao Butter is just better Nutella. To make a simple, unflavoured nut butter, you can use raw, roasted or activated (see below) nuts and blend them to a butter as these methods explain. A little salt and sometimes a splash of water are good additions.

You can make these with raw nuts and they will be delicious, but for maximum nutrition I recommend activating them. To do this, soak them overnight in cold water, drain and rinse, then dry out in the oven at its lowest temperature (70 °C/50 °C fan/gas as low as it will go) for 4 hours, until completely dry. A good trick here is to leave the oven door slightly ajar so all the moisture can escape. Activating your nuts sounds a bit silly, but it is basically a way of boosting their

nutritional value. First you soak them in water, which tricks the nuts into thinking they are about to grow into a plant and means that all their nutrients are released. Then you gently heat them to dry them out, so that they can be kept for longer – the soaked nuts only last a couple of days.

For a really smooth nut butter you will need a good food processor or high-speed blender. If you don't have one of these, a crunchy texture can be achieved using a hand blender.

....

Get all your ingredients together for whichever nut butter you are making. If using coconut oil, melt it and let it cool. A hot spoon will help you measure the coconut oil more easily.

Place the nuts in your food processor or blender and blitz until you have a fine powder. You will need to stop the food processor and use a spatula to scrape down the sides from time to time. This should take 2–4 minutes, depending on how powerful your blender is. If you like your nut butter crunchy, spoon out 2 heaped tablespoons before it's completely smooth, to stir through at the end.

Once the nuts begin to form a paste, add the rest of the ingredients except the water and blend until you have a smooth butter – you may need to scrape down the sides again a few times.

Add the water and blend again. Top up with a little extra water if necessary, until your nut butter is the consistency you like. Scoop out of the processor; if you have reserved some crunchy nuts, put the nut butter into a bowl, add the crunchy nuts and beat together. Then spoon the butter into sterilised jars (see page 257). Keeps in a cool place for up to 6 weeks.

COCONUT AND CARDAMOM ALMOND BUTTER

300g raw skin-on almonds (activated if you like – see introduction)

100g creamed coconut (½ a block)

50g coconut sugar

2 tablespoons lucuma powder (optional)

1 teaspoon vanilla extract

the seeds from 4 cardamom pods, bashed

the seeds from 2 vanilla pods

100–150ml water

....

HAZELNUT AND CACAO BUTTER

300g raw skinned hazelnuts (activated if you like – see introduction)

4 tablespoons maple syrup

4 tablespoons coconut oil or cacao butter

4 tablespoons cocoa powder or cacao nibs

100–150ml water

....

SALTED DATE CARAMEL PECAN BUTTER

300g raw pecans (activated if you like – see introduction)

10 stoned medjool dates

a good pinch of salt

100–150ml water

Blood orange
and double chocolate
rye muffins

This is Terry's Chocolate Orange in a healthier muffin version that you can happily eat for breakfast. Either you are with me on this one, or you'll have already turned the page.

These little guys have no refined sugar, no dairy and just a bit of spelt flour. You could easily use a good gluten-free flour if you preferred, which works really well, as the milk and oil stop the muffins drying out.

I have kept these pretty lean, but if you wanted to make them more of a treat, 100g of chopped dark chocolate sprinkled over at the end would add some gooey melting goodness. I use blood oranges when they are in the greengrocer's, but a normal orange will work just fine too.

....

Preheat the oven to 220 °C/200 °C fan/gas 7. Line a muffin tin with paper liners. Get all your ingredients together. If you are using coconut oil, melt it and let it cool.

Sift together all the dry ingredients in a large mixing bowl.

Crack the eggs in a separate bowl and whisk together, then add the milk, maple syrup and oil while constantly stirring. Grate in the zest of one of the oranges.

Use a knife to cut the peel from both oranges and remove any pithy bits, then chop the oranges into small pieces, taking care to cut out any bits of white pith from the centre.

MAKES 12 MUFFINS

150ml olive oil or coconut oil

150g good white spelt flour

50g wholegrain rye flour

5 tablespoons cocoa powder
(I use the raw stuff)

1 teaspoon baking powder

3 free-range organic eggs

250ml milk of your choice
(I use drinking coconut milk)

150ml pure maple syrup

2 unwaxed blood oranges or
normal oranges

100g dark chocolate (70%)

Add the dry mixture to the wet mixture. Roughly chop the dark chocolate and add half of it to the batter, along with half the orange pieces. Use a spatula to carefully fold everything together until combined.

Divide the batter between the muffin tins and top with the rest of the dark chocolate and orange pieces. Bake for 16–18 minutes. Best warm from the oven.

Malted chocolate buckwheat granola

My formative years in America led to an obsession with malted chocolate milkshakes. In fact malted chocolate anything. I don't go for the milkshakes much any more, but I still crave that chocolate and malt combo. This is my solution, a health-packed granola, which has the kickback of creating a chocolate malt milkshake in the bottom of my bowl.

You can use more maple syrup in place of the barley malt here, but I love the malty taste that it adds. Barley malt syrup can be found in all health food shops and is a naturally processed sweetener, made up of about 50 per cent maltose, a sugar which is only about one-third as sweet as white sugar. It still retains many nutrients from the barley grain from which it was made, and this type of complex sugar takes longer to digest, so it won't give you the sugar highs and lows of a Mars bar.

This granola is great for a quick sweet snack – I eat it on its own with almond milk and a scattering of raspberries – but it's just as good with yoghurt or on top of a bowl of porridge to liven things up a little.

....

Preheat the oven to 180°C/160°C fan/gas 4 and get all your ingredients together.

In a generously sized bowl, mix the oats, buckwheat, dried fruit, cocoa powder and chia seeds. Roughly chop the pecans and add these too.

Put the maple syrup, barley malt syrup and coconut oil into a pan and warm through.

Pour the syrup mixture over the oat mixture and mix until it's all coated. Then put on a large baking tray or two smaller ones and squish it all together with your hands to form little bundles of granola.

MAKES A GOOD JARFUL (ABOUT 800G)

300g rolled oats
200g buckwheat
100g dried fruit (I use coconut, chopped dates, raisins or chopped apricots)
4 tablespoons cocoa powder
30g chia seeds
125g pecans
60ml maple syrup
4 tablespoons barley malt syrup
60ml melted coconut oil

Put into the oven for 5–10 minutes, then take the granola out and use a spoon or spatula to roughly break it up a bit. Put back into the oven for a further 5–10 minutes.

It's done when it starts to form lovely crunchy bundles. The dark colour from the cocoa will mean it's easy to overcook, as you won't be able to see, so if anything take it out a little earlier if you think it's ready.

Start as you mean to go on cereal

I make this cereal blend and keep it in a big jar in my kitchen, so that when mornings are short, rushed, bleary or fraught I know that I can scoop some of this into a pan and 15 minutes later have something fortifying and nourishing which will set me up for the rest of my waking hours. I often use rye flakes or even buckwheat in place of the oats.

If I can, I try to soak my cereal overnight in a little water with a squeeze of lemon juice. If you don't remember, or you think that's a bridge too far, don't worry about it.

I have given three ideas for toppings below, two sweet, one savoury, all delicious.

. . . .

FOR THE MIX
Mix all the ingredients in a large jar, or mix in a bowl and divide between two smaller jars, and store for up to 3 months.

TO COOK
Mix about 50g of the mixture (about ¼ of a cup per person) with 250ml of water or a mixture of water and unsweetened almond milk. Bring to the boil, then simmer for 20 minutes until cooked and creamy.

MAKES ABOUT 20 PORTIONS

1 cup (90g) oats (gluten-free if needed)
1 cup (200g) millet flakes
1 cup (170g) quinoa flakes
1 cup (190g) amaranth
¼ cup (40g) chia seeds
¼ cup (30g) poppy seeds

TOPPING IDEAS
· Sliced persimmon, pomegranate, dates and chopped pistachios
· Grated apple, nutmeg, cinnamon and chopped almonds
· Poached egg, chilli and toasted sesame seeds

Ultimate pecan banana breakfast bread

This is my ultimate banana bread. Soft, squidgy and light all at once, with a topping of seeds that would make any Swedish baker proud and studded with chunks of darkest chocolate. All without any gluten or dairy or refined sugar. So toast this for breakfast with wild abandon and congratulate yourself for making something that is insanely indulgent-tasting and incredibly delicious without dragging you down.

This bread is also just as good and a bit more virtuous without the chocolate. I add chocolate if I'm making it for teatime but otherwise I leave it out and it becomes our breakfast for the week. Much better than a piece of toast or a bowl of porridge. If you can't find coconut sugar you could use light soft brown sugar here.

Preheat the oven to 170°C/150°C fan/gas 3 and get all your ingredients together. Grease a 900g non-stick loaf tin with coconut oil.

While the oven comes up to temperature, roast the pecans in it for 10 minutes, then roughly chop and set aside. Meanwhile, blitz the oats in a food processor until you have a scruffy flour. Put the oat flour into a bowl.

Put the bananas into the food processor with the 100g of coconut sugar, maple syrup, almond milk and melted coconut oil and blitz until well combined. Add the oat flour, baking powder and a good pinch of salt. Blitz until combined, then stir in the pecans. Add the caraway seeds, if using.

Pour half the batter into the loaf tin. Break the chocolate up into thin strips and lay it along the middle of the batter, leaving space at the end. Pour in the rest of the batter and top with the extra spoonful of coconut sugar. Bake for 1 hour 10 minutes, or until a skewer comes out clean. Leave to cool on a wire rack for at least 30 minutes.

MAKES 1 GOOD 900G LOAF

75ml melted coconut oil,
plus extra for greasing

200g pecans (walnuts work too)

200g rolled oats

4 large ripe bananas

100g coconut sugar, plus 1 tablespoon (optional)

100ml maple syrup

100ml unsweetened almond milk

2 teaspoons baking powder

a good pinch of caraway seeds (optional)

75g dark chocolate (70%)

Make your own chickpea tofu

It can be hard to get your hands on really good tofu. A few small producers have started making good tofu in the UK, but, by and large, the tofu sold in our supermarkets is pretty average. I think part of the reason many people turn their noses up at it is because they haven't had the good stuff.

As we all know, much soy is grown in very industrialized, often GM, farms, so, in my quest to throw the nutritional net as wide as possible, I looked to chickpeas here. Chickpea tofu is a staple of Burmese kitchens. It's more flavourful than regular tofu, but is still neutral enough that it could be paired with Asian, Indian or even Italian flavours.

This recipe does take a bit of planning, as the chickpea flour needs to soak for 1–2 days. It also makes a big, family-size amount. If there are only a couple of you in the house, I'd suggest halving the quantities.

....

In a very large saucepan (one that will take about 4 litres), combine the chickpea flour and water. Place a clean tea towel over the top and leave it to sit somewhere not too warm, where it will not be disturbed. Let it sit for about 24 hours; you may need to soak it a little less in a warmer climate.

After the soaking time, uncover the saucepan; the chickpea flour will have started to ferment a little, so there may be a slight fermentation smell. Without stirring or moving the saucepan, carefully remove 1 litre of water from the top of the mixture with a ladle or measuring jug and discard.

In a medium pan, melt the oil over medium heat. Carefully pour in the remaining liquid, without disturbing the bottom too much and stopping when you get to the thick chickpea paste at the bottom. This

MAKES ABOUT 1.5KG

FOR THE BASIC TOFU
350g chickpea flour
3.5 litres cold water
½ tablespoon coconut oil
2½ teaspoons fine sea salt

OPTIONAL FLAVOURINGS
Smoked
replace the salt with smoked salt

Spiced
1 tablespoon ground turmeric
1 teaspoon ground coriander

Herbed
a small bunch of fresh thyme,
leaves picked and very finely chopped
a small bunch of fresh oregano,
leaves picked and very finely chopped

paste stays in the saucepan and it'll be what you will use to thicken the mixture shortly.

Add the salt and a flavouring if you are using one, and whisk well to combine. Cook over a medium heat, stirring frequently, for 15–20 minutes, until the mixture begins to simmer and thicken.

Add the chickpea paste from the saucepan and keep stirring vigorously with a wooden spoon. After about 6–7 minutes, the mixture will thicken to the consistency of a cake batter. Cook for a further 10 minutes to cook out the flour; you'll need to keep stirring to stop the bottom burning.

Line a 20cm × 30cm baking tray with a clean cotton tea towel or cheesecloth. Pour the thickened chickpea mixture into the baking tray and smooth the surface. Fold the edges of the cloth over the top and let it sit at room temperature for about 6 hours.

To remove the tofu from the tray, place a chopping board on top and flip it over, then pull the cloth away. Cut into meal-sized chunks of about 200g each and keep in the fridge for up to 5 days. Keep the tofu on a tray as it can let out a little water while it's stored in the fridge. Unfortunately, this tofu doesn't freeze too well.

To fry your chickpea tofu, use a non-stick pan and a little oil to stop it sticking – it is a little bit more prone to sticking than normal tofu.

Perfect home-cooked pulses

Cooking dried pulses may not sound like the most enchanting or exciting thing to do in a recipe, or even anything new. But cooking pulses this way has seriously changed how I do things in my kitchen, how delicious my meals are, how much time it takes to put them together and how much they cost.

Pulses are an amazing ingredient to include in your diet. They are high in complex carbohydrates and fibre, high in protein and low in fat, while being loaded with vitamins.

I have moved from using tinned pulses to cooking my own, from scratch, in big batches and freezing them cleverly in portions, ready to make into hummus, soups or stews. They are so much more delicious and buttery cooked at home, and the process is one I love – running your hands through a bowl of dried beans is so satisfying, as is opening a freezer drawer packed with ready-to-go little bags of beans.

It is worth mentioning that the length of time it takes to cook a dried pulse will depend on how long ago it was dried. The older it is, the longer it will take to cook. I would encourage you to buy pulses from places where they are less likely to have been sitting around for a long time; supermarkets and anywhere that has loose pulses to buy by weight are good options.

If you want to find out more about pulses, get yourself a copy of the brilliant book *Pulses* by Jenny Chandler, which is a pulse bible and has inspired some of the techniques below.

A note on beans and protein. The protein we get from beans is not a complete protein like the ones found in eggs, quinoa, buckwheat and chia seeds. Pulses have only seven of the eight amino acids which make up a complete protein. But the missing piece of the jigsaw

can be filled by grains or sesame seeds, which contain the eighth amino acid. So eating your pulses with a little bread (see page 212) or in hummus (with tahini see page 257) will form a complete protein, which will provide more energy and nourishment for your body.

....

SOAKING

Most beans will benefit from a little overnight soak in double their volume of fresh cold (ideally filtered) water. Soaking pulses makes them much easier to digest and reduces their famous side-effects as well as their cooking time; it also allows them to cook more evenly. If you don't have time to soak them, don't fret, as there are a couple of other options.

Either give them a quick soak, for as much time as you have but ideally for 2 hours, or cook them without soaking – though in my experience the time you save by not soaking them will only be replaced by the extra time they take to cook.

COOKING

To cook, drain the soaked pulses, put them into your largest pan, and cover with cold water to come about 3cm above the level of the pulses. Bring to the boil, then boil steadily for 5 minutes (10 for kidney beans) – this is important, as it deactivates the toxins in the pulses – and after that turn down the heat to a very gentle simmer and cook until tender and creamy. Cooking on a low heat like this will make sure the skins stay intact and that they cook evenly. It is better to shake your pan rather than stir with a wooden spoon, as stirring will break the skins of the pulses.

A cooked pulse should remain intact but should collapse into a buttery, creamy mush when squeezed. Chickpeas will remain a little harder but should still be soft throughout.

I season my pulses once they are cooked, as seasoning them while cooking is said to toughen the pulses and give them a powdery texture. They do need a good bit of seasoning once they come off the heat.

FREEZING

You can freeze your cooled pulses in their cooking liquid, in portions as they would come in a tin, but I prefer to freeze them without their liquid. I season them well, then drain the liquid and allow the pulses to cool before freezing them in meal-sized bags. If I have time I freeze them on a tray first, to stop them sticking together, and bag them up once frozen.

SOAKING AND COOKING TIMES FOR DRIED PULSES

....

QUICK

SOAK 30 MINUTES + COOKING 30–40 MINUTES

Lentils and split peas
Moth beans
Mung beans

....

SHORT

SOAK 2–3 HOURS + COOKING 30–40 MINUTES

Aduki beans
Black-eyed beans

....

MEDIUM

SOAK 4 HOURS + COOKING 1–1½ HOURS

Borlotti beans
Butter beans
Cannellini beans
Haricot beans
Kidney beans
Pinto beans

....

LONG

SOAK 8 HOURS OR OVERNIGHT + COOKING 1½–3 HOURS

Chickpeas
Fava beans
Soya beans

Amazing grains

Grains and so called pseudo-grains like quinoa and amaranth (which look and cook like grains but are actually seeds) are a big part of how I like to eat, but quite a few of them take a while to cook, so I like to cook them in big batches and have them in my fridge or freezer to have to hand for whenever I need something quickly.

Eating a range of grains means that you are introducing a wide spectrum of vitamins and minerals into your diet.

These days you can also buy packets of pre-cooked grains in supermarkets and delis, though they vary wildly in quality and in what has been added to them. Some brands, like Merchant Gourmet, are pretty reliable and have very little else added – if you check the packet carefully these can be a good option if you are in a fix.

SOAKING

These grains and pseudo-grains, like pulses and nuts, will benefit from soaking. It will speed up their cooking time, maximise their nutritional value and make them easier to digest. An overnight soak in double the amount of cold (ideally filtered) water is ideal, but a couple of hours is good too – and if you don't have time it's not the end of the world.

COOKING

Drain your soaked grain and put into a large pot with the specified amount of liquid. I cook all my grains in vegetable stock, which adds flavour and depth. I often also squeeze the juice of a lemon into the pan, then put the squeezed halves into the pan while the grain cooks to add extra flavour. Cook until tender.

STORING AND FREEZING

Drain your grains and cool well – if you want to speed this up you can cool them on a couple of baking trays. They can then be stored for 3–4 days in the fridge, or frozen in portions for super-quick dinners.

QUINOA – RED, BLACK AND WHITE

You'll need 2 mugs of water to 1 mug of quinoa. I like to dry toast my quinoa in a pan before cooking until it starts to make a popping sound – this adds a deeper, toasty flavour. Cook for about 12 minutes, until all the water has been absorbed and the little curly grain has popped out. I like to keep the pan on the heat until I can just hear the popping sound again, to make sure all the water is gone.

BROWN RICE

Rinse your rice under running cold water. For 1 mugful of rice you'll need 1¼ mugs of water for long-grain and 1½ for wholegrain. Bring to the boil, then reduce to a steady simmer and cook for 30 minutes, until the rice is tender. Drain and leave in the pan to steam for a further 10 minutes.

AMARANTH

You'll need 2½ mugs of water for every mug of amaranth. Bring to the boil, then simmer for 20 minutes until the grains are fluffy and the liquid has been absorbed.

BUCKWHEAT

Buckwheat comes in two forms: kasha, which is toasted, and buckwheat groats, which are untoasted. I usually use the raw groats. First rinse your groats under running cold water until it runs clear. Then you'll need 2 mugs of liquid for each mug of groats. Bring to the boil, then simmer for 20–30 minutes, until tender, 15–20 if you use toasted buckwheat or kasha. If you like, you can toast the groats yourself, in a dry pan for 1–2 minutes until they smell nutty.

MILLET

You'll need 2½ mugs of water for every mug of millet. Bring to the boil, then simmer for 25 minutes until the grains are fluffy and the liquid has been absorbed. Fluff up with a fork. You can toast millet to add a nutty flavour in the same way as quinoa.

FARRO

You'll need 2 mugs of water to every mug of farro. Bring to the boil, then simmer for 30 minutes, until tender. Farro contains gluten.

PEARL BARLEY

You'll need 3 mugs of water to each mug of barley. Bring to the boil, then turn the heat down and simmer for 45–50 minutes, until tender. Pearl barley contains gluten.

FREEKEH

Freekeh is immature wheat that is harvested while still young and soft, then roasted or sun-dried. The health bonus of harvesting immature wheat is that it retains more of its nutrients and proteins than its fully-grown counterparts. It even claims to have fewer carbohydrates than regular wheat because it's young.

Wash the grain first by swirling in water and rubbing the grains together vigorously. Drain and repeat until the water is clear. You'll need 2 mugs of water for every mug of freekeh. Bring to the boil, cover, and simmer until the water is completely absorbed (about 15 minutes for cracked grain and 45 minutes for wholegrain). Remove from the heat and use a fork to fluff up.

Quick home-made paneer

This is one of the most pleasing things to make at home – the white curds wrapped in muslin are so satisfying in their clean white simplicity.

I like making my own paneer, as that way I can use really good organic milk. Home-made paneer is a good bit cheaper than shop-bought stuff and, of course, the flavour and texture are much more delicate. If you are making paneer for a crowd you can double this recipe, but this makes a perfect amount for a meal for four.

MAKES ABOUT 400G

2 litres full-fat organic milk
the juice of 2 lemons

Pour the milk into a high-sided saucepan and place over a medium heat. Bring to the boil, stirring every now and again so the milk doesn't form a skin.

Meanwhile, place a piece of muslin or a clean tea towel over a large bowl and set aside.

When the milk starts to boil and to rise in the pan, add the lemon juice and stir until all the milk curds have formed. Remove from the heat and use a slotted spoon to scoop all the curds out of the milk into the muslin or cloth. Bring the edges of the muslin together in your hands, then twist and carefully squeeze out any excess moisture from the curds.

Lay the tea towel bundle on a plate and squash down with something heavy; I use a large pestle and mortar. Leave for 40 minutes to set and you are ready to cook.

If you are not using the paneer straight away, place it in a bowl and cover with water. Pop it into the fridge – it will keep for up to 5 days.

A Sunday vat of soup

Life is busy, and even as someone who spends their life cooking I often don't take as much time as I would like to make sure I am really well nourished. Some weeks I am saintly; I get in a rhythm and make breakfasts, lunches and dinners to be proud of. Other weeks I don't do so well; it's in those weeks that I always try to make a pot of soup, and it's not always on a Sunday. I make it in my biggest pot so that we can have eight servings of easy goodness throughout the week.

This soup has a simple, nourishing character to it. It's made from sweet potatoes and squash, which are good sources of the kind of carbohydrates our bodies love, and are packed with beta-carotene and vitamins too. I pair them with fennel seeds, which help with digestion, and some chilli to boost the metabolism and warm.

From one soup there are a million things you can do. I find it difficult to eat the same thing night after night, so I use the soup as the base for a few different meals, adding different toppings and extras each night to make it seem new. Below are a few ideas of how to make one pot of soup into lots of different dinners.

The first day I tend to eat it blitzed and smooth, straight up with a quick herb oil and some bread. The second night I eat the soup with texture – I add some tinned cannellini beans and top with some chopped chilli. The next night I serve it with brown rice, yoghurt, coriander and green chilli. The possibilities are endless, and if you do get bored you can freeze it in portions for a quick dinner when time is tight.

Fill and boil a kettle and get all your ingredients together. Get your biggest pot out – if you don't have a big enough pot, two smaller ones will do.

Wash and finely slice the leek, and finely slice the onion, carrots and celery.

Heat a large pan on a medium heat and add a little olive or coconut oil. Once the pan is hot, add the chopped veg and cook for 10–15 minutes, until soft and sweet.

Meanwhile, peel the sweet potatoes and chop into large chunks. Deseed the squash and roughly chop into similar-size chunks (I leave the skin on, but if you like you could peel this too).

Once the vegetables are soft and smelling good, add the sweet potatoes, squash and spices along with 2 litres of hot water from the kettle and the veg stock powder or cube. Bring to the boil, then turn down to a simmer and cook for 30–40 minutes, until the vegetables are soft and falling apart, topping up with a little hot water from the kettle if it starts to look a little thick.

I cool the lot and store it in the fridge or freezer until I'm hungry. I store it all without blitzing – I like to eat it both silky smooth and with a more stew-like texture, so I warm and blitz it in portions as I need.

HERE ARE SOME OF THE WAYS I LIKE TO EAT MY VAT OF SOUP

- Whizzed until smooth, topped with a quick basil oil and served with good bread.
- Stew-style, with some cannellini beans added while warming and topped with crispy fried thyme breadcrumbs and red chilli.
- Half whizzed, warmed and served on brown rice with chopped chilli, coriander, lime zest and a spoonful of yoghurt.
- Stew-style, with some smoked paprika stirred in while warming and topped with broken corn tortillas, red chilli and some little bits of avocado.

SERVES 8

1 leek

1 red onion

2 carrots

2 sticks of celery

olive oil or coconut oil

2 medium sweet potatoes

1 medium butternut squash

1 tablespoon fennel seeds

1 tablespoon Turkish chilli or a good pinch of red chilli flakes

1 tablespoon vegetable stock powder or 1 stock cube

Making good vegetable stock

This recipe is one from *A Modern Way to Eat*. It's a favourite in my house and still my preferred way to make stock. I use marigold bouillon when I'm in a fix but I always try to have a jar of this in the fridge to ladle into soups and broths.

You'll need two big 1 litre preserving jars that will fit into your fridge. Don't feel tied to the amounts of veg below – the great thing about stock is that you can use up all the trimmings and odds and ends you have in the fridge. Just work to the same ratio, half-filling your litre jars with veg.

Fill up the kettle and boil it. Divide the chopped veg and other ingredients between your two 1-litre jars. Fill the jars with the just-boiled water, leaving a couple of centimetres gap at the top – each jar should hold about 750ml. Pop the lids on and leave in a safe place to cool down.

When cool, sieve straight away for a light veg stock, or put into the fridge for 12 hours and then sieve for a more full-bodied stock.

Once sieved, pour the stock back into the jars and store in the fridge, where it will keep for up to a week.

MAKES 2 LITRES

2 carrots, roughly chopped

1 red onion, cut into wedges

1 leek, cut into rounds

2 sticks of celery, roughly chopped

2 bay leaves, scrunched

a small bunch of fresh thyme

1 teaspoon sea salt

a few black peppercorns

Honeyed rye bread

I can't live without a good loaf of bread in the house. Real bread and gluten get shunned as unhealthy and out of bounds for a lot of people, who are trying to eat consciously and healthily. I believe that a good, carefully made loaf of bread is a joy we should never try to live without (unless of course we have a serious intolerance). Many people's bad reaction to bread could be because of the quality of the bread they are eating. Like anything else, a good loaf needs good ingredients, some time and a lot of love.

I believe in varying the grains I eat, and I find wholegrain flours more delicious and much more nourishing. So here is my current favourite loaf, half spelt and half rye, with a little honey, lots of seeds and some caraway on top if that's your thing. Slicing a just-warm loaf of home-made bread satisfies and nourishes me in a way a thousand green juices couldn't.

Get all your ingredients together. Put the flours into a warm, generously sized mixing bowl with the salt and mix well.

Mix 300ml of hand-hot water with the honey and yeast, stirring to dissolve. Leave for a couple of minutes, until bubbles rise to the top, then pour into the flour. Mix first with a fork, then with your hands, until you have a sticky dough, and tip on to a floured board or work surface. Form the dough into a ball, then knead by hand, pulling and stretching the dough for a good 4 or 5 minutes. If you have a stand mixer with a dough hook you can use it to get the dough to this point.

Lightly oil the bowl, then return the dough to it, cover with a tea towel or clingfilm and set aside in a warm place for about an hour, until the dough has risen by half (it won't rise as much as a normal loaf because of the rye flour).

MAKES 1 GOOD LOAF

250g rye flour
250g spelt flour
1 teaspoon fine sea salt
3 tablespoons runny honey
7g sachet of dried yeast
50g seeds (I use poppy and sunflower)
1 tablespoon caraway seeds (optional)

Remove the dough from the bowl, place on a lightly floured board and knead again, briefly, for just a minute or two, adding and kneading in the seeds as you go.

Shape the dough into a flat oval and put it on an oiled baking tray. Cover with the tea towel again and leave to rise once more for 30 minutes or so, until it has risen by half again. Preheat your oven to 240°C/220°C fan/gas 9.

After 30 minutes, slash the top of the dough in a criss cross with a sharp knife and scatter over the caraway seeds.

Half fill a deep baking tray with boiling water and place on the bottom of your oven. This will create steam as the loaf bakes and help give your bread a lovely crust and texture.

Now bake the loaf in the oven for 30–35 minutes, until golden all over. Be really careful when you open the oven door, as some hot steam may come out. To check if your bread is ready, lift it up and give it a tap on the bottom. If it sounds hollow, like a drum, it's good to go. Cool on a rack so the bottom keeps its lovely crust.

How to make tahini

I am in love with tahini; I think there are very few things that a spoonful of tahini doesn't improve. It has been almost canonised in my house, where I have a couple of different types on the go at any time. I use it in smoothies, on porridge and pancakes, in soups, dressings and stews and spread on toast topped with banana. I like the deep, nut-butter-style sweetness and its toasted earthiness.

There are many different types of tahini out there, ranging from the more liquid, lighter, sweeter Middle Eastern ones made with hulled sesame seeds to the health food-shop, deep brown, raw, unhulled kind.

My favourite tahini is made from toasted unhulled sesame seeds. Toasting sesame seeds actually makes them easier to digest, improves their flavour and makes them sweeter.

Unhulled sesame seeds, like wholegrain wheat, have their outer casing intact. This outer bit holds quite a few of the nutrients, so see if you can search them out; though if you can't, the hulled whiter seeds will do fine. Black sesame seeds will work just the same here too, and make an amazing, dark, rich tahini.

A note on sterilising jars. Rather than boiling jars to sterilise them, warm them in the oven while you are working. Heat the oven to 140°C/fan 120°C/gas 1. The jars should be in there for 10 minutes minimum, but can stay in longer. This process eliminates boring boiling and washing. The hottest cycle on your dishwasher will do the trick too, just make sure you fill the jars while they are still quite hot.

This will make a 200–250g jar.

....

If you like your sesame seeds roasted (they usually are in tahini) put 200g sesame seeds into a dry frying pan over a medium heat, stirring them to prevent them burning, until they are lightly toasted (not too dark) and fragrant; this will take about 5 minutes. Transfer the toasted sesame seeds to a large plate and let them cool completely.

Place the sesame seeds in a food processor. Blitz for 2–3 minutes, until the seeds form a crumbly paste. Add 2 tablespoons of mild olive oil (or other mild-flavoured oil, such as grapeseed or untoasted sesame) and blitz for a couple of minutes more, scraping down the sides as necessary, until the mixture forms a thick and fairly smooth paste. For thinner tahini, add more oil, 1–2 tablespoons at a time, and process until the desired consistency is reached. Season well with sea salt and blitz again.

Transfer the tahini to a sterilised jar or other airtight container. Store in the fridge for a month or longer. If the mixture separates, just stir it well.

Three vibrant dips

These are three quick and easy dips that I keep in my fridge in rotation. They are great for boosting quick meals and for quickly slathering on sandwiches. But more than anything, these are what I snack on: I dip a cracker (see page 260) or a carrot into whichever of these happens to be in the fridge. With these in my kitchen my 4 p.m. raid of the biscuit tin is often avoided.

2 cloves of garlic
200g red lentils, rinsed
juice of ½ a lemon
2 tablespoons tahini
a good pinch of dried chilli
1 tablespoon olive oil

TO SERVE
2 tablespoons toasted sesame seeds
chopped herbs or cresses (I used baby amaranth)

RED LENTIL AND LEMON HUMMUS
Bash the garlic and put into a small pan with the rinsed lentils. Cover with cold water and cook the lentils until tender and mashable, then drain and remove the skins of the garlic. Blitz the lot until whipped and smooth, add all the other ingredients and blitz again. Top with the toasted seeds and the herbs.

1 × 250g packet of cooked vacuum-packed beetroots
4 dates
2 tablespoons regular or coconut yoghurt
a small bunch of fresh dill
1 unwaxed lemon
1 tablespoon olive oil
a handful of toasted walnuts

BEETROOT, WALNUT AND DATE
Blitz the beetroots, dates, yoghurt and half the bunch of dill with the zest and juice of the lemon and the oil, and season well with salt and pepper. Throw in the toasted walnuts and blitz again, keeping a bit of texture if you like; I like mine smooth.

200g frozen peas
a small bunch of fresh coriander
a small bunch of fresh mint
1–2 green chillies
2 unwaxed limes
20g from a block of coconut cream

INDIAN GREEN PEA
Fill and boil a kettle and get your ingredients together. Cover the peas with boiling water and put aside for a few minutes. Finely chop the coriander and mint and put into a bowl. Finely chop the green chillies, zest of both limes, and add both to the bowl, along with the juice of one of the limes. Season well with salt and pepper. Drain the peas and mash well, then add them to the herbs. Grate over the coconut cream and mix well.

Amazing crackers

These easy crackers are perfectly snappable and are loaded with seeds and goodness. They are naturally wheat-free and can easily be gluten-free too if you use gluten-free oats. I keep a tin of these on hand for snacks and dipping. They last for ages and are really good for little people too – just leave the salt (and chilli) out.

Most often I make these straight up with sea salt, but I have given a couple of flavouring options, one super savoury and one sweet. Pretty much any dry spice would work here, so experiment with your favourites.

....

Preheat your oven to 190°C/175°C fan/gas 5. Get all your ingredients together, and line two baking sheets with greaseproof paper.

Combine all the dry ingredients, including one of the optional flavourings if you are using them, and stir well. Mix the maple syrup, coconut oil and water together in a measuring cup. Add to the dry ingredients and mix very well, until everything is completely soaked and the mixture becomes very thick.

Divide between the two lined trays and even out a bit, then put another piece of greaseproof on top. Use a rolling pin to roll out the mixture until it is about ½cm thick. Take the top layer of greaseproof off and use the tip of a sharp knife to score the mixture into rectangles.

Bake the crackers for 20 minutes. Remove from the oven and flip the sheet over, then peel off the greaseproof to expose the underside of the crackers. Put back into the oven for another 20 minutes. They are ready when they are firm and golden round the edges.

Allow to cool, then break along the lines where they have been scored.

MAKES ENOUGH FOR 1 WEEK'S SNACKING

100g sunflower seeds
100g pumpkin seeds
100g sesame seeds
50g poppy seeds
50g chia seeds
200g rolled oats
1 teaspoon sea salt
1 tablespoon maple syrup
3 tablespoons melted coconut oil
350ml water

OPTIONAL FLAVOURINGS

1 heaped teaspoon fennel seeds and a pinch of dried chilli

or

1 tablespoon raisins, roughly chopped, and a pinch of cinnamon

Coconut yoghurt

This requires some patience but it's much cheaper than buying pots of coconut milk yoghurt, which are super-expensive. Use the best pure coconut cream you can get, organic if possible.

Probiotics help your gut. You can use a pot of normal yoghurt here if you are not bothered about it being dairy free.

....

First sterilise your jars. I do this by putting them through the hottest cycle of my dishwasher or into the oven at 170°C/150°C fan/gas 3 for about 20 minutes.

Place the packet of coconut cream, still in its plastic wrapper, into a bowl of hot water to soften for 10–15 minutes. Once softened, massage the coconut with your hands to get rid of any lumps then squeeze out into a bowl. Whisk 350ml boiling water into the coconut cream, taking care to whisk out any lumps. Once cooled to hand temperature, stir in the powder from the probiotics and transfer to a jar.

If the weather is warm, leave the yoghurt in a warm spot in the house for 12–24 hours. Otherwise you can put it into the oven at the lowest possible temperature for 8–10 hours.

Chill the yoghurt for at least an hour, until it has cooled and has begun to thicken. It will thicken more as it is stored in the fridge, where it will keep for about 10 days.

MAKES 2 GOOD-SIZED JARS

200g block of full-fat coconut cream
2 probiotic capsules

Home-made milks from nuts, oats and seeds

I have up to four different types of milk in my fridge at any one time, usually a small carton of organic milk, almond milk, oat milk and often drinking coconut milk. I like to vary the kinds of milk I use, to make sure I am getting as much nutrition as possible and to make the most of the flavours of each individual milk. Almond milk for coffee and baking, oat milk for hot chocolate, coconut milk for granola and a jot of organic cow's milk for tea.

It is easy, more nutritious and much cheaper to make your own non-dairy milk at home. All you need is a decent blender and a nut-milk bag (a muslin bag made for draining nut milk) or, failing that, a piece of muslin or a fine, thin tea towel.

These milks can be made from most nuts and seeds, and some grains. My favourites are almonds, pistachios, walnuts, hazelnuts, macadamia nuts, cashew nuts, sunflower seeds, pumpkin seeds, sesame seeds, hemp seeds and oats. Below is a universal recipe that can be used for any of these. It works on ratios rather than weight, so I use a US cup measure, but if you don't have one of these don't worry – a heaped tea or coffee cup will work fine.

I have also included some of my favourite flavoured milks, which I make from time to time to mix things up a bit.

EASY HOME-MADE MILK

Take 1 cup of your chosen nut and place in a bowl. Cover with a cup of cold (ideally filtered) water and leave to soak for 8 hours; this will allow the nut to release all its nutrients and maximise the goodness in your milk.

Once the soaking time is up, drain the nuts and place in a blender, discarding the soaking water. Add 4 cups of fresh cold (ideally filtered) water to the blender and blitz until you have a thin, smooth, cloudy mixture.

Put a muslin bag or cloth over the mouth of a jug and pour the nut milk through. Allow it to sit and drip into the jug for 5–10 minutes, then use your hands to squeeze out as much moisture from the nuts as you can.

Pour the milk into a clean bottle; it will keep in the fridge for 3–4 days. The leftover nut pulp can be added to hummus or can be used in place of ground almonds in baking.

ALMOND, TURMERIC AND HONEY

Follow the recipe above, using almonds. Before blending, add a pinch of ground turmeric, a pinch of ground cardamom and a tablespoon of honey to make a beautiful yellow milk.

SESAME, DATE AND CINNAMON

Use sesame seeds to make your milk, and before blending add 4 pitted medjool dates and a pinch of cinnamon.

OAT AND MAPLE

Use ½ a cup of oats and ½ a cup of pecans to make your milk and add 1–2 tablespoons of maple syrup before blending.

LEMON ZEST AND VANILLA

Use pistachios to make your milk and add the zest of ½ a lemon and a drop of vanilla essence before blending.

Rainbow paletas

All over Mexico there are shops dedicated to Mexican ice lollies called paletas. They are filled with a few deep glass-topped chest freezers, where a rainbow of cheery paletas line up like a frozen sweet shop.

They come packed with just about anything you can think of: strawberry, mango, guava, avocado, pineapple, watermelon and horchata were my highlights, each in almost neon brilliance. I must have eaten at least one a day. The Mexican ones are made with barely smashed fruit and lots of sugar.

These are my version, all good stuff and a bit of natural sweetness packed into an ice lolly so you always have a nourishing sweet treat at your fingertips.

I encourage you to taste the lolly mixtures before you freeze them to check for balance, sweetness and sourness. Do remember that they will taste subtler and less sweet once frozen.

---

2 ripe avocados
300ml coconut water
the juice of 1 lemon
the seeds from a vanilla pod, or 1 teaspoon vanilla paste
1 teaspoon runny honey

AVOCADO, HONEY, VANILLA
De-stone the avocados and scoop the flesh into a blender. Add all the other ingredients and blitz until smooth. Taste for sweetness and add a little more honey if needed. Pour into moulds and freeze for at least 4 hours.

300g cucumber
a bunch of fresh mint
100ml elderflower cordial
the zest and juice of 2 unwaxed limes
a good swig of gin (optional)

ELDERFLOWER, CUCUMBER, LIME
Put the peeled and roughly chopped cucumber and the leaves from the mint into a blender and blitz for a few seconds, so that a little texture remains. Pour into a bowl and add the cordial, lime zest and juice and, if you like, a good swig of gin. Taste and adjust the lime or sweetness if needed. Pour into moulds and freeze for at least 4 hours

350ml unsweetened almond milk

6 dates

the seeds from a vanilla pod, or 1 teaspoon vanilla paste

2 tablespoons maple syrup

DATE, ALMOND MILK, MAPLE

Put all the ingredients into a blender and blitz until the dates are well puréed. Pour into moulds and freeze for at least 4 hours.

200g strawberries

50ml agave syrup

100ml coconut water

the zest and juice of 1 unwaxed lemon

½ teaspoon bashed fennel seeds

STRAWBERRY, LEMON AND FENNEL SEED

Hull the strawberries and put them into a blender. Blitz until you have a rough purée, then tip into a bowl and mix in the agave syrup, coconut water, lemon zest and juice and the bashed fennel seeds. Pour into moulds and freeze for at least 4 hours.

Carrot cake flapjack bars

I'm not sure what my favourite cake is. It's a toss-up between a lemon drizzle, a carrot cake and my ginger, molasses and apple cake, but it's safe to say carrot cake always makes the top three. Here I've brought together carrot cake and another favourite thing, flapjacks. The first time I made flapjacks I was open-mouthed as I mixed so much butter and sugar into the oats. A lot of my friends still eat them, thinking they are a healthy treat; a few oats will fool anyone. These little squares, however, are sweetened with some dried fruit and maple syrup, and, as sweet things go, they are fairly virtuous.

Sometimes I mix up the spices here and use a little cardamom in place of the cinnamon.

....

Preheat the oven to 200°C/180°C fan/gas 6.
Get all your ingredients together. Soak the chia seeds in 4 tablespoons of water in a little bowl. Melt the coconut oil.

Line a 20cm × 30cm baking tray with baking parchment. Put the oats into a food processor and blitz until you have a scruffy flour, then tip the oat flour into a large mixing bowl.

Put half the dried fruit into the food processor and blitz until it is broken down and a little mushy. Scrape into the bowl with the oats.

Peel and grate the carrot and the apple (no need to peel) into the large mixing bowl and add the coconut, chia mixture, pumpkin seeds, maple syrup, vanilla, spices and melted coconut oil. Mix well.

Spoon into a baking tray, smooth over the top with the back of a spoon, and bake for 40–45 minutes, until golden brown. Allow to cool a little in the tray, then completely on a rack, and slice into 16 pieces.

MAKES 16

4 tablespoons chia seeds

50g coconut oil

200g rolled oats

150g dried fruit (I use a mixture of dried apricots and raisins)

1 medium carrot

1 apple

100g desiccated coconut

100g pumpkin seeds

4 tablespoons maple syrup

1 tablespoon vanilla extract

½ teaspoon ground cinnamon

a pinch of ground ginger

Summer rhubarb
and strawberry crisp bars

Just-right sweet yet tart scarlet and vibrant pink summer fruit sits on top of a half-pastry, half-flapjack base, all topped off with a crunchy crumble topping. These bars are free from eggs, dairy and refined sugar, and gluten-free if you use a good gluten-free flour blend.

If coconut sugar and oil are too much of a stretch for you, follow the recipe using the same quantities of butter and soft, light brown sugar. You can vary the fruits you use here depending on the time of year: apples and blackberries are great, as are plums and pears. In the summer, apricots and raspberries are amazing.

Preheat the oven to 210°C/190°C fan/gas 7 and get all your ingredients and equipment together. Line a roughly 30cm × 20cm baking tray with greaseproof paper and rub with a little coconut oil.

Put the coconut oil or butter into a large saucepan over a medium heat and leave to melt, then take off the heat. Add the oats, flour, 150g sugar and a pinch of salt and give it a good mix. Take out 6 tablespoons of the mixture and put to one side to make the topping. Press the rest of the mixture into the bottom of the baking tray. Press down with the back of a spoon until it evenly coats the tray.

Chop the rhubarb and the strawberries quite finely and put into a bowl; squeeze over the lemon juice, add 1 tablespoon of sugar and toss to coat. Scatter the fruit over the crumb base then sprinkle with the reserved topping. Bake for 40 minutes, until the fruit is bubbly and the crumbs are golden.

Let the bars cool in the tray (you can do this in the fridge to speed things up), then cut into roughly 20 pieces. Store in the fridge – they will keep for 4–5 days.

MAKES 20 BARS

150g coconut oil or butter, plus extra for greasing
150g rolled oats
150g spelt flour
150g coconut sugar or unrefined light brown sugar, plus 1 tablespoon
250g rhubarb (about 2 medium stalks)
300g strawberries, hulled
the juice of 1 lemon

Amazing lemon cannellini cake

A cake made of beans? I thought it sounded absolutely rubbish too. But I gave it a go anyway, and when a springy, light, well-crumbed sponge appeared 30 minutes later it was a revelation.

This cake is pretty great. It's totally grain, gluten, refined sugar and dairy free and it tastes as indulgent and amazing as any cake should.

I made a candied lemon topping. It's pretty easy, but if you don't have the time or the inclination, a good grating of lemon zest will do. To make the candied lemon peel, peel the zest off a lemon, drop it into boiling water for a couple of minutes, then transfer to a pan and add a couple of tablespoons of maple syrup. Place over a high heat for a couple of minutes, until the peel becomes translucent. Transfer to a greaseproof-lined plate and don't touch until it's cool.

Preheat the oven to 190°C/170°C fan/gas 5. Get all your ingredients together, and grease and line a 20cm springform cake tin. Drain the cannellini beans.

In a food processor blitz the drained beans, honey and vanilla seeds until smooth, then add the eggs one by one, pulsing as you go. Tip the whole lot into a mixing bowl and gently fold in the ground almonds, baking powder, melted coconut oil and a pinch of salt. The batter may be a little looser than you'd expect from a cake batter, but don't worry.

Pour the mixture into the prepared tin and bake for 30–40 minutes. The cake is ready when it is golden brown on top, firm to the touch and a skewer comes out clean.

For the icing, put all the ingredients into a blender and blend until very smooth and shiny, scraping down the

SERVES 8–10

FOR THE CAKE
2 × 400g tins of cannellini beans
150ml set honey
the seeds from 1 vanilla pod
4 free-range or organic eggs
100g ground almonds
2 teaspoons gluten-free baking powder
100g melted coconut oil
a good pinch of sea salt

FOR THE LEMON ICING
200g silken tofu
2 tablespoons melted coconut oil
the juice and zest of 1 unwaxed lemon
2 tablespoons set honey
1 teaspoon orange blossom water

sides from time to time if you need to. This will take about 3–4 minutes. Transfer to a bowl and pop into the fridge to set while the cake is cooking and cooling.

Once the cake has had its time, take it out of the oven, leave it to cool for 5 minutes in the tin, then cool completely on a rack.

Once cool, top with the icing and either grate over more lemon zest or finish with the candied lemon (see the introduction).

Sweet potato and malted chocolate cake

I think every cook needs a good chocolate cake up their sleeve. I have spent years chasing my dream chocolate cake and for the time being this is it. A double-layered, light as a feather chocolate sponge, sandwiched with a foolproof icing.

I use sweet potato here to add natural sweetness and for a squidgy but perfectly light and bouncy well-crumbed cake. The sweet potato means that you need less sugar and less butter, but there is no compromise on flavour

The icing is based on the famous Brooklyn blackout cake, though mine is a good bit less heavy-duty than the original. You cook the icing like a custard, which makes it really easy to work with when cool and amazingly glossy and rich, like a chocolate ganache but without being loaded with cream.

SERVES 10–12

200g sweet potatoes
275g plain spelt flour
½ teaspoon ground cinnamon
4 tablespoons good-quality cocoa powder
2 teaspoons baking powder
a pinch of fine sea salt
100g good-quality Greek yoghurt
150g butter or coconut oil, at room temperature
150g soft light brown sugar or coconut sugar
1 teaspoon vanilla extract
3 large free-range or organic eggs

FOR THE CHOCOLATE CUSTARD ICING
75g cornflour
600ml unsweetened almond milk
300g golden caster sugar or coconut sugar
2 tablespoons barley malt extract
100g good-quality cocoa powder, sifted
1 teaspoon vanilla extract

Preheat your oven to 200°C/180°C fan/gas 6 and get all your ingredients together. Grease two 20cm springform tins and line the bases with greaseproof paper.

First make the sweet potato purée. Peel and roughly chop the sweet potatoes, then steam or boil them until cooked. Drain, reserving the cooking water, then purée them in a blender or mash them really well until smooth, adding about 4 tablespoons of the cooking water to loosen a little.

Sift the flour, ground cinnamon, cocoa, baking powder, and salt into a bowl. In a separate bowl mix together the sweet potato mash and the yoghurt.

Using a stand mixer, or a bowl with a hand-held electric mixer or some elbow grease, cream together

the butter and sugar until pale and fluffy. Stop occasionally to scrape the mixture off the side of the bowl with a spatula. Add the vanilla, then mix in the eggs one by one. Add the dry ingredients and slowly mix until just combined – don't overwork it. Fold in the sweet potato and yoghurt mixture, then divide evenly between the two lined tins. Bake on the middle shelf of the oven for around 35 minutes, until cooked through – a skewer inserted into the centre of the cake should come out clean. Leave the sponges to cool in the tins for 5 minutes, then transfer them to a rack to cool completely.

Meanwhile, make your chocolate icing. Blend the cornflour with about a third of the almond milk, until smooth. Bring the remaining almond milk to the boil in a small non-stick saucepan with the sugar, barley malt and cocoa, whisking until smooth. Add the cornflour mixture and bring to the boil, stirring constantly, until you have a rich, thick custard. Remove from the heat, add the vanilla extract and stir well. Ideally the mixture should be silky smooth, but if not, give it a quick whiz in a food processor. Pour into a large bowl, cover the surface with clingfilm and put into the fridge to cool completely.

To assemble, cut each of the cakes in half and give the chocolate-custard filling a stir. Spread the filling over one of the cake layers, taking it almost to the rim, then place another cake layer on top and repeat until you have the four layers stacked, with the best-looking layer on top. Coat the top of the cake with the remaining custard icing and let it drizzle down the sides.

super-fast
breakfasts

Breakfast is my favourite meal and, for me, eating a good breakfast is how I set my intentions for the day. My mornings, like most people's, are rushed but these breakfasts can be put together quickly, and there are a couple of slightly longer ones for the weekend. Goodness-packed acai bowls, fluffy almond milk French toast, easy favourite smoothies, 10-minute pancakes, avocado fritters and quick but delicious porridge.

10 MINUTES

Acai bowls

I ate these like they were going out of fashion one summer in Brazil, and they are still one of my favourite things to start the day with. In the healthy eating world smoothie bowls have become quite a thing, but this is the original. It is eaten cold, which I don't mind in summer or winter.

Acai berries have been called superfoods for the high levels of nutrients they contain. They are jam-packed with antioxidants, amino acids and omega fatty acids. In the UK it's pretty hard to come by them frozen, let alone fresh, so I've used acai powder here. Acai powder isn't the cheapest, but for the amount of nutrition it provides your body I think it's a good investment. These bowls can be made with just the frozen berries if acai powder eludes you.

This recipe uses frozen bananas. Freezing bananas is a great way to make use of any that are going unloved in your fruit bowl. Make sure you peel them first. I cut mine into 2cm chunks and put them into a sandwich bag; I then lay the filled and sealed bag flat in the freezer, spreading the banana pieces out so they don't stick together.

....

Get all your ingredients together.

Place the banana, berries, acai powder, honey and most of the milk in a blender and blitz until creamy and smooth, adding more milk to thin the mixture if needed. Aim for a thick, almost ice-cream-like consistency. If you don't have a stand-up blender, a good hand blender, a jug and a bit of determination will work fine.

Spoon the acai mixture into bowls and top with your choice of toppings and pretend you are on Ipanema beach.

MAKES 2 BOWLS

1 large banana (frozen if possible – see introduction)

200g fresh or frozen berries (2 handfuls)

3 tablespoons acai powder

1 teaspoon runny honey

100ml your choice of milk (I use unsweeteend almond)

TOP WITH ANY OF THE FOLLOWING

granola

seeds (I use hemp and pumpkin)

bee pollen

goji berries

chopped almonds

desiccated coconut

honey

nut butter

10 MINUTES

Almond milk, ricotta and lemon French toast

The quickest and most indulgent breakfast I know. It's usually saved for weekends as it's more substantial than my weekday breakfast, but is easily quick enough for a weekday.

I love the simple flavours here: vanilla, lemon and creamy ricotta. I like to use good sheep's ricotta if I can get my hands on it. The rest of the tub is great stirred through pasta or spread on toast and topped with berries.

I have found that decent gluten-free bread works really well too, as the almond milk mixture helps prevent the bread from being too dry. For vegans you can make the French toast with extra almond milk and skip the eggs and use some coconut yoghurt in place of the ricotta.

Get all your ingredients and equipment together.

Break the eggs into a bowl and whisk in the almond milk and vanilla. Pour into a deep baking tray and lay all four slices of bread in the mixture. Leave to soak for a minute.

Put a pan on a medium heat and add a good knob of coconut oil or butter. Turn the bread over and leave for another minute to soak up the mixture, then carefully lower into the pan and cook for 2–3 minutes on each side until golden and crisp, taking care when you flip it, as the bread will be quite delicate.

Pile two slices on each plate, dot with ricotta and grate over the zest of the lemon. Top with honey, if you like things sweet.

SERVES 2

2 free-range or organic eggs

125ml unsweetened almond milk

the seeds from 1 vanilla pod, or 1 teaspoon vanilla paste

4 thick slices of good bread or brioche

a knob of coconut oil or butter

2 tablespoons good ricotta cheese

1 unwaxed lemon

runny honey, to serve (optional)

Strawberry, coconut and cardamom smoothie

This smoothie is bliss. It is comforting, refreshing and nourishing all at once. I often find green smoothies or juices a bit hard to handle in the morning. I crave something milky. I first made this drink one summer in California, and I think I must have had it for breakfast every day for the following two weeks. The coconut and almonds mean it's packed with protein and good fats.

I love the depth the cardamom brings but, if you are not a fan, a pinch of ground cinnamon will work well too.

It's important to note that the coconut milk I use for this smoothie is the stuff for pouring over your cereal, not the stuff in a tin, which would be too rich and thick. Coconut water also works well.

MAKES 1 LARGE BREAKFAST GLASS OR 2 SMALLER ONES

4 tablespoons desiccated coconut

a handful of strawberries or frozen berries

200ml drinking coconut milk or almond milk

a small handful of almonds

the seeds from 1 cardamom pod

1 teaspoon light agave syrup or runny honey

Put all the ingredients into a blender and blitz until smooth and frothy. You will need a good blender to whiz up the coconut and almonds completely. If yours is less powerful, blend for longer until it is completely smooth. If your smoothie looks too thick, add a little ice-cold water bit by bit until you have the consistency you like.

Pour into a tall glass and drink while pretending to be on a beach.

morning smoothies

Smoothies are my favourite way of getting goodness into my body when time is short. If you are really bad in the mornings (like me), you can prep the jug of ingredients the night before and leave it in the fridge overnight. I've left quantities a little vague here, as you will want to tweak to your taste. You can make these smoothies a bit thicker and serve them in a bowl topped with fruit, or add-ons (see below). In the winter frozen fruits are always in my freezer; they are cheaper than fresh, they taste great and they make lovely thick smoothies. I like my smoothies with a little ice – though not too cold. You can't go wrong if you follow this sort of template.

FAVOURITE ADD-ONS

LUCUMA   This super fruit from Peru is high in anti-oxidants and minerals and beta-carotene.

MACA   This comes in a powdered form and is thought to calm the nervous system and help our bodies cope with stress. Look for 100% maca root when you are buying it.

HEMP   Comes in seed and powder form and is one of the only complete plant sources of protein. It is also high in omega 3 and 6 and in fibre.

BEE POLLEN   This is an incredible whole food – providing almost every nutrient, mineral and vitamin our bodies need. It is powerful stuff, so start with just a teaspoon a day.

SPIRULINA AND CHLORELLA   These are two types of algae, which are insanely rich in protein and nutrients. This stuff is like a natural green caffeine.

CREAMY FRUIT
Banana, avocado
(40%)

BACK-UP FRUIT OR VEG
Strawberries, apples, spinach
(20%)

FLAVOURING
Vanilla, lemon, tahini
(spoonful)

SWEETNESS
Date, maple syrup, honey
(dash)

PROTEIN BOOST
Soaked seeds, soaked nuts, protein
powder, nut butter
(tablespoon)

LIQUID
Plant milk, coconut water
(40%)

FAVOURITE SMOOTHIES

MANGO SESAME
boosts calcium, anti-inflammatory
Frozen banana · Mango or persimmon ·
Turmeric · Tahini or sesame seeds ·
Lime · Almond or plant milk

CHOCOLATE SHAKE
Frozen banana · Avocado · Cacao ·
Maple syrup · Plant milk

GINGER PEAR REFRESHER
Avocado · Green apple or pear ·
Celery · Mint · Ginger · Coconut water

CARROT AND GINGER
high in vitamin C, anti-viral
Frozen banana · Apple, carrot ·
Orange · Lemon · Ginger · Plant milk

MAGENTA
Strawberries · Raw beetroot ·
Pomegranate · Dates · Ginger ·
Coconut water

GOOD GREENS
electrolytes, protein,
good after workout
Frozen banana · Celery · Kiwi ·
Avocado · Hemp seeds · almonds ·
Coconut water

STONE FRUIT
Peach · Apricot · Plum · Berries ·
Vanilla, acai · Plant milk

LEMON VANILLA, LAYERED
vitamin C, antibacterial,
aids digestion
Bottom layer · raspberries and
maple syrup · blitz and pour into
glass · **Top layer** · frozen bananas ·
vanilla · zest of ½ a lemon · honey ·
coconut milk

PEANUT BUTTER AND STRAWBERRY, LAYERED
Bottom layer · strawberries, lime
juice and honey · blitz and pour
into glass · **Top layer** · banana ·
vanilla · peanut butter · plant milk

Tahini-drizzled super fruit

SERVES 2

FOR THE TAHINI DRESSING
4 tablespoons tahini
2–4 tablespoons runny honey, to taste
juice of 1 lemon
a good pinch of ground cinnamon

FOR THE FRUITS
2 bowls of seasonal fruits:
spring – Alphonso mango, blood oranges, strawberries
summer – raspberries, peaches, apricots, cherries
autumn – pears, plums, blackberries, figs
winter – apples, pears, persimmons, pomegranates
2 tablespoons seeds (hemp, sesame and sunflower work well)
2 tablespoons goji berries or raisins

Having the same thing every morning seems a waste of a golden opportunity. I like to mix up what I have for breakfast just as I would my lunch or dinner. And breakfast has to start me off on the right foot. Bright-coloured food packed with goodness, but it has to fill me up or I get grumpy.

This is what I make when I want a bowl of fruit. It is a true fruit salad in that it even has a dressing. The dressing sweetens the fruit a little, which I love, as sometimes I find it too acidic to eat first thing, and it also adds a kick of morning protein.

If you are a tahini lover like me, give this a try. If you are less convinced about tahini you could swap it for almond butter for a more mellow dressing.

....

Get all your ingredients together.

Put the dressing ingredients and a couple of tablespoons of cold water into a jar with a screwtop lid and shake until well combined.

Wash and chop the fruit and arrange in bowls. Top each bowl with a spoonful of seeds and berries and drizzle with the tahini dressing.

10-minute pancakes

These are a fast-forward version of my favourite ever pancakes. This time the whole process is done in a blender, but if you don't have one you can make these with oat flour instead of the oats and ground almonds instead of the whole nuts, and mash the banana well.

I use a teacup for measuring to save time in the mornings. The pancakes may vary a little from cup to cup but it's really the ratio that makes this recipe work, so don't worry.

Since they are sweetened with natural nutrient-rich bananas and maple syrup and use whole grains instead of flour, you can happily eat these pancakes with gusto.

....

Get all your ingredients and equipment together.

Put the oats into a blender and blitz until you have a rough scruffy flour. Grate the apple. Put the nuts, milk, apple and banana into the blender and blitz until combined.

Heat a non-stick pan on a medium heat and add a little coconut oil or butter. Allow it to melt, then add ladlefuls of the pancake batter to make Scotch pancake rounds. Cook for 2–3 minutes, or until bubbles rise to the surface. Use a spatula to carefully flip the pancakes over and cook on the other side. The first batch are always more delicate, so don't worry if they look a bit scruffy. Keep them warm while you cook the rest.

Once all your pancakes are done, use a speed peeler to peel your apples into long pieces then put into a bowl and toss with the lemon juice, the cinnamon and nutmeg.

Serve the pancakes stacked and topped with the apple, maple syrup and, if you like, a little yoghurt.

MAKES 6 PANCAKES

1 teacup of oats (about 80g)

1 apple

½ a teacup of nuts (about 50g) – pecans or almonds (for kids use another ½ cup of oats)

1 cup or about 150ml of milk of your choice (I use unsweetened almond)

1 medium banana

coconut oil or butter, for frying

TO FINISH

2 apples

the juice of ½ a lemon

a pinch of cinnamon

a tiny grating of nutmeg

honey or maple syrup

yoghurt of your choice (I use coconut)

Nordic morning bowls

I have come to think of porridge in the same way I think of soup – a wonderful warming bowl of gentle goodness – but that's not enough for me; I like texture changes and flavour pops in my food, so just as I spend a few extra minutes thinking about how to create toppings, texture and flavour for a bowl of soup, I have started to do the same for my bowls of porridge.

I tend to eat porridge when it's cold, so Nordic spices and wintry vibes are what I want.

If you can think ahead, putting the oats, milk and spices into a bowl and then into the fridge overnight will help make the oats easier to digest and save you time in the morning. Just pour into a pan when you're ready to make your porridge. This works well with quinoa flakes or millet flakes too.

....

Get all your ingredients and equipment together.

Put the oats and milk into a saucepan with 125ml of cold water and a pinch of salt and start to warm it over a medium heat. De-stone and roughly chop the dates and add to the pan with all the spices and the vanilla.

Stir the porridge and cook until it is thick and creamy. Once you've got it to the consistency you like, take it off the heat and spoon it into deep bowls, adding a squeeze of honey if you like your porridge sweet. Top with a spoonful of almond butter, a scattering of raisins and hemp seeds, a spoonful of coconut yoghurt and a good grating of apple. Hand-warming bowls of good stuff.

SERVES 4

200g rolled oats
300ml milk of your choice
(I use unsweetened almond)
2 dates
a pinch of ground cinnamon
a pinch of freshly grated nutmeg
a pinch of ground cardamom
1 teaspoon vanilla extract

TO TOP
honey (optional)
2 tablespoons almond butter
a handful of raisins or currants
a scattering of hemp seeds
coconut yoghurt
1 apple

overnight oats

Overnight oats are what I often make when
I know my morning will be rushed. They are so
easy, and take 2 minutes to throw together the
night before. I find them particularly useful when
I'm going on a long journey or travelling. If you
are grabbing them to take to work or on a plane
or train, mix them in a screw-top jar so they are
ready to go. Frozen fruits work well here, as they
are cheaper than fresh and defrost in the fridge
overnight. For all these recipes, follow the ratio
below for 2 servings, mix all the ingredients
in a bowl or jar and leave in the fridge overnight.

- **GRAIN (100G)** • oats, rye flakes, quinoa flakes

- **LIQUID (330ML)** • plant milk, water, coconut milk

- **SEEDS (2 TABLESPOONS)** • pumpkin, flax, chia

- **SWEETNESS (DASH)** • maple syrup, vanilla

- oats • chia • coconut milk • desiccated coconut, honey, mango

- oats • chia • almond milk • vanilla, strawberries

- oats • chia • plant milk • bashed cardamom, honey, raspberries, lemon zest

- quinoa flakes • chia • nut milk • lemon zest, berries

- oats • plant milk • banana, raisins, almonds, peanut butter

- buckwheat • hemp • plant milk • figs, apple, cinnamon

- oats • chia • almond milk • maple syrup

- oats • vanilla, dates, figs, nutmeg, maple syrup, cinnamon

- oats • flax • nut milk • vanilla, plums, maple syrup

- oats • chia • vanilla, lemon, peaches, maple syrup

Peach and raspberry ripple breakfast

This breakfast is a quick one, but it does call for you to soak the oats overnight so that it's soft enough to blend. It's really easy – I am not super-organized and I don't remember to do this all the time, but when I do it feels satisfying.

I eat this cold, and for me it's a summer alternative to porridge, which I only really eat on the coldest days of the year. If you like you can warm it a little, though it does lose some of its raw credentials.

This recipe is inspired by one on one of my favourite blogs My New Roots by Sarah Britton, who has been flying the flag for inspired plant-based eating long before it was so mainstream. Sarah uses buckwheat instead of oats which is also delicious. She also inspired me to swirl my breakfast like raspberry ripple ice cream or a 1980s dessert plate.

....

Get all your ingredients together. Cover the oats with warm water and the lemon juice or vinegar and let it sit overnight. Next morning, drain the oats and rinse very well.

In a blender, food processor, or high-speed blender (this works the best) blend the raspberries, peach flesh and maple syrup until they are liquid. Spoon out about half into a bowl and set aside.

Leave the remaining purée in the blender and add the drained and rinsed oats and the rest of the ingredients. Blend on the highest setting until it's really smooth and silky. Taste and add a little maple syrup if you like things sweeter.

Serve the porridge in bowls or little glasses, with the raspberry and peach purée swirled in. Leftovers keep in the fridge for up to 2 days.

SERVES 3–4

1 cup oats
the juice of ½ a lemon or 1 teaspoon apple cider vinegar
2 tablespoons chia seeds
125ml milk of your choice, or water
1 frozen banana
1 vanilla pod, seeds scraped

FOR THE RASPBERRY AND PEACH RIPPLE
200g raspberries (fresh or frozen, organic if possible)
1 peach
1 tablespoon maple syrup

Avocado fritters

These cloud-like bright green fritters are polenta-crusted and, if you are an avocado fan, I think you should run into the kitchen and make them right away. I thought I'd had avocado in every way possible until I ate these. My dear friend Emily and I whipped these up one morning while trying out recipes for this book.

I top these vivid fritters with a quick cashew hollandaise and sometimes a poached egg, but I leave the egg out if I'm making this for my vegan brother and sister and they love it just as much.

These are a great way to use avocados that are a little overripe, and a brilliant way to use up cooked quinoa. I always have some cooked quinoa in the freezer (see pages 246–7), which makes this even faster.

SERVES 4

FOR THE FRITTERS
75g quinoa or 150g cooked quinoa
4 avocados
1 unwaxed lime
100g kale
1 green chilli
a bunch of fresh coriander
150g polenta
coconut oil
4 free-range or organic eggs (optional)

FOR THE HOLLANDAISE
150g cashews
½ teaspoon ground turmeric
the juice of 1 lime
1 tablespoon olive oil

Fill and boil a kettle and get all your ingredients and equipment together. Put the cashews into a heatproof bowl and cover with boiling water from the kettle.

If you need to, cook your quinoa. Weigh it out in a mug or measuring jug, making a note of the level it comes to, rinse well in cold water then pour it into a large saucepan. Fill the mug to the same level with boiling water and add to the pan, then repeat so you have double the volume of water to quinoa. Cook for 10–12 minutes, until translucent and the little curly grain has popped out. Once cooked, drain well and leave to cool slightly.

While the quinoa is cooking, get on with some other jobs. Peel and de-stone the avocados, then mash roughly, still leaving some texture and a few lumps. Grate over the zest of 1 lime, then squeeze in the juice and mix well.

Wash the kale, then tear off and discard the stalks. Tear the leaves into small pieces. Finely chop the green chilli, then cut the stalks off the bunch of coriander and finely chop the leaves.

Add the kale, chilli and coriander to the bowl of avocado, along with the cooked and drained quinoa and a good pinch of salt and pepper, and mix well.

Divide the mixture into 8 and shape into 8 patties. Pour the polenta on to a baking tray and spread it out into one thick layer. One by one, lay each fritter on top then sprinkle some polenta from the tray generously over the other side. Pop into the fridge to set while you make the hollandaise.

Drain the soaked cashews, mix the turmeric with 3 tablespoons of hot water, then put both into a food processor with the lime juice, oil and a good pinch of salt. Blitz until smooth and glossy – this will take a little longer if your blender is not a high-speed one. You can also use a hand-held blender.

Heat a pan on a medium heat, add a little coconut oil, and fry the patties until golden on both sides. You can either use two pans here or you can fry in batches, keeping the cooked fritters warm in a low oven.

If you are topping your fritters with a poached egg, now is the time to poach them, while the fritters are frying. Everyone has their own method – I drop them into a just simmering shallow pan of water for 3–4 minutes, depending on the temperature of the eggs and how runny I want them.

Serve two fritters each, with a poached egg, if that's your thing, and plenty of hollandaise. Take to smiling faces at the table.

Golden turmeric milk

I am a hot drink person. I love tea in all its forms: Earl Grey in the morning, fennel, rose, cinnamon, camomile, you name it. The bit of work surface next to my kettle is piled high with jars of petals and flowers from far-flung places, caddies of tea and carefully chosen occasional coffee. But when the nights draw in I like something more comforting, and this is my new blanket of a drink.

Its sunny yellow colour brightens up my mornings. The spices calm and soothe my bedtimes. I try to have a little turmeric every day, usually in a tea, because its healing and anti-cancer properties have been widely celebrated. I love its saffron-toned vibrancy and its like-nothing-else taste, so it's not a hardship by any means.

I prefer not to have too much dairy, especially before bed, so I make this with unsweetened oat or coconut milk. I make a peppy morning version with a little bashed ginger in place of the cinnamon too. Allowing the milk to cool a little before you add the honey will stop the heat damaging the nutrients in the honey.

....

FOR 1 CUP

2 cardamom pods
200ml unsweetened oat, coconut, almond or any milk you like
¼ teaspoon ground turmeric
¼ teaspoon ground cinnamon
1 teaspoon runny honey

Bash the cardamom pods in a pestle and mortar and put into a small saucepan with the milk, turmeric and cinnamon. Heat gently until it is almost boiling, but don't let it boil, otherwise, if you are using a non-dairy milk, your milk may split.

Pour into a mug (you can pour through a strainer if the cardamom seeds bother you) and, once it has cooled a little, stir in the honey and drink, making sure not to spill any, as its lovely yellow colour can be rather persistent.

Red quinoa porridge

My sister Laura and I have always been joined at the hip. We have the same voice, mannerisms and sense of humour and we chat every day, even though she lives on the other side of the world. While I was writing this book my sister was camped out in Peru, overloading on her favourite food, quinoa, and buying piles of alpaca blankets she'll probably regret when she gets home. This porridge was inspired by a picture Laura sent me from a café.

If you are avoiding gluten you can leave out the oats here; they add a little creaminess to the porridge, so you may need to cook it for a little longer to get it really creamy without.

Here I top my porridge with mango, coconut, dates and lime, but you could vary the fruits and use whatever is in season. My favourites are:

spring – poached apricots, saffron, pistachios
summer – strawberries, vanilla, lemon
autumn – plums, oranges, cinnamon
winter – blood oranges, dates, pomegranates

SERVES 2

100g red quinoa
(or white, or black)
50g rolled oats
150ml unsweetened
almond milk
a pinch of cinnamon
2 dates

TO SERVE
1 mango
a few more dates
coconut yoghurt
coconut flakes
1 unwaxed lime

Put the quinoa, oats, almond milk and cinnamon into a pan with 100ml of cold water and bring to a simmer over a medium heat. De-stone and chop the dates and add them to the pan for sweetness.

Cook for 10 minutes, until the quinoa has softened and cooked and the curly quinoa grain is visible. Make sure you stir every so often so it doesn't stick.

Meanwhile peel and chop the mango and roughly chop a few more dates. Once the porridge is cooked and the consistency you like, spoon it into bowls, pile on the mango, dates, yoghurt and coconut flakes, and finish with a good grating of lime zest.

quick puddings and sweet treats

I love puddings and I often reach for something sweet mid-afternoon. These puddings and treats are made with unrefined sugars, oats, nuts and seeds and the odd bit of chocolate. The puddings come together in minutes, while the treats take a little longer to make but will sit happily in a tin to satisfy those sweet cravings throughout the week.

Saffron apricots

The quickest, most exotic-tasting pudding I know, made mainly of things that sit happily in your cupboard.

I usually use the deep, dark, unsulphured apricots, as I find them more delicious and easier to digest. The cooking time for these will depend on how soft your apricots are – some are only semi-dried and will cook quicker than the harder, fully dried ones, so adjust your cooking time accordingly.

I use orange blossom water here to add a heady fragrant taste, which I love. If you can't find it, it will work without.

I serve these with a spoonful of coconut yoghurt or good thick Greek stuff, and they are equally good on top of some vanilla ice cream. I love the dairy-free Booja-Booja one.

SERVES 2

100g dried apricots
a good pinch of saffron strands
the juice of 2 oranges
1 tablespoon orange blossom water
a couple of teaspoons runny honey
chopped pistachios or almonds
(optional)

Put the apricots into a small pan with the saffron and orange juice and bring to a simmer. Simmer for 5–10 minutes, until the apricots have softened. Scoop the apricots out and put the orange and saffron back on the heat to reduce a little. This will take a couple of minutes.

Allow to cool before spooning the apricots and syrup into bowls. Daintily drizzle over the orange blossom water and squeeze over a little honey. Top with yoghurt and some chopped pistachios or almonds, if you like.

15
MINUTES

+
CHILLING
TIME

Raw cookie dough bars

I make batches of these in rotation with my raw brownies from *A Modern Way to Eat*. They sit in a tin in the fridge for times when only a hit of something sweet will do. They are one of those magical things that are as delicious as they are good for you.

Raw cookie dough from the bowl was one of my favourite childhood sneaked treats, along with that Ben and Jerry ice cream that has thick chunks of cookie dough peppered through it. This is my new cookie dough, in a bar, just as delicious.

....

Line an approximately 20cm square brownie tin with greaseproof paper.

First put the Brazil nuts into a food processor and blitz until they are a fine flour – don't over-blitz or they will become nut butter. Add the honey, coconut sugar, coconut oil and vanilla and pulse gently until the mixture just comes together in a ball. Roughly chop the chocolate into small pieces.

Turn out the dough on to a chopping board and scatter over the chopped chocolate, then use your hands to gently but quickly knead in the chocolate and distribute it through the dough.

Press the mixture into a lined baking tray and pop into the fridge for a few minutes. The longer you leave them, the firmer they will be before cutting – 10 minutes will do, but 30–40 minutes is ideal. Cut into 16 pieces and store in the fridge.

MAKES 16 BARS

200g skinned Brazil nuts
4 tablespoons runny honey
2 tablespoons coconut sugar
3 tablespoons coconut oil
the seeds from 1 vanilla pod,
or 1 teaspoon good vanilla extract
100g dark chocolate
(70% is good here)

Coconut and goji fudge bites

I spent three school holidays working at my local farm shop. All the other people my age were on the tills, or at the pick-your-own huts, weighing up punnets of just-picked strawberries and raspberries. But I got the best job by a mile: I was in charge of sweets and fudge.

On my first day I was led into a room with a bin full of sweets, presented with a huge fudge kettle and given the fudge recipe, and told I had a free rein to experiment and make any flavour I wanted! It was to this day one of the best jobs I can imagine. My experiments were endless: raspberry and cardamom fudge in summer, blackberry and bay fudge in autumn and mulled wine brown sugar fudge at Christmas.

This is my nod to those days of carefree fudge-making, though after months of making the stuff and unwrapping thousands of packets of butter I favour a fudge made from more virtuous ingredients. This is a brilliant gift for anyone, but especially for someone who's feeling under the weather, as these little fudge bites are packed with goodness.

Goji berries have a lovely flavour, sweet and tangy, and a striking colour. On top of that they are one of the kings of the food world – they are a complete protein, so they're great if you eat a completely vegetarian diet, and one of the highest antioxidant foods in the world.

MAKES 24 BITES

200g cashews

100g desiccated coconut

zest and juice of 1 small
unwaxed lemon

¼ teaspoon ground cardamom

the seeds from 1 vanilla pod, or
1 tablespoon good vanilla extract

3 tablespoons thick set honey

4 tablespoons coconut milk
or water

50g goji berries

Fill and boil a kettle and get all your ingredients and equipment together. Weigh out all your ingredients. You'll need a food processor, a mixing bowl and a small deep container for the fudge. Line your container with greaseproof paper.

In a food processor, blend the cashews, coconut, a good pinch of sea salt, lemon zest and cardamom until you have a fine powder. It's important that it's a powder, as otherwise the fudge will be grainy. If you have a less powerful food processor this may take a few minutes.

Once you have a fine powder, add the vanilla, honey and lemon juice and blitz until it comes together into a ball. Add the coconut milk and blitz again.

Pour some hot water over the goji berries and leave for 30 seconds to soften a bit, then drain really well and pat dry with kitchen paper.

Scoop the fudge mixture into your lined container and push it down with the back of a spoon to even it out to a 1.5cm-thick layer. Scatter over the goji berries, put into the fridge to firm up for about 20 minutes, then cut into little squares.

Rhubarb, apple and maple pan crumble

I love desserts but I'm not much of a planner, so it's rare unless I have people round that I think to make them in advance – most of the time they are a quick reaction to a craving for something sweet after dinner. So, while I love a crumble, I really only make them on a weekend after a big family meal. This is a crumble you can make any night of the week and it's filled with good nutrient-packed stuff and natural coconut sugar, so you can eat it with a smile.

Any orchard fruit or stone fruit would work well here. I like plums and pears in autumn and apricots and apples in summer. Dried fruits like prunes work well too. And, if you like, a swig of sloe gin or Armagnac would do nicely too. If you can't get coconut sugar, a soft light brown sugar will work but it won't be as virtuous.

....

SERVES 2 GENEROUSLY

FOR THE FRUIT
200g apples (about 2)
200g rhubarb
2 tablespoons coconut sugar
the juice of ½ an orange

FOR THE CRUMBLE TOPPING
a small handful of skin-on almonds (about 45g)
5 tablespoons small oats
1 tablespoon coconut sugar
a knob of coconut oil or butter
1 tablespoon maple syrup

Get all your ingredients together and put two frying pans on a medium heat.

Peel the apples and chop into thin slices, then trim the rhubarb and chop it into slices about the same size. Put both fruits into one of the pans with the sugar and the orange juice and cook for 5 minutes, until soft but still holding their shape.

Roughly chop the almonds. Put the oats and almonds into another pan and toast on a low heat for a few minutes. Add the sugar and stir until the sugar starts to melt a little, then quickly take off the heat and add the coconut oil or butter, and the maple syrup.

Spoon the fruit into bowls and top with a sprinkling of the crumble. Serve with custard or yoghurt; I like coconut yoghurt.

Chocolate and Earl Grey pots

These are ten-minute chocolate puddings that are unreasonably delicious considering how little effort goes into making them. They are rich, creamy and custardy, with a subtle back-note of Earl Grey.

They use tofu as a base. If you think that's weird, you won't be alone, but it makes for a creamy, incredibly delicious pudding without having to pour in half a tub of cream.

Instead of Earl Grey you could add all sorts of other flavourings here, such as the zest and juice of an orange or a lime and a shot of rum or even brewed and strained green tea.

Be sure to buy good-quality organic silken tofu for this; it usually comes in a small sealed Tetrapak. The firm stuff won't work. The quality of tofu you buy is important, as soy crops are some of the most modified and messed around with on the planet; if you can, buy organic or, even better, UK-made – there are a couple of makers in the UK flying the flag for good tofu.

This recipe can easily be doubled or tripled if you are feeding a crowd. And these pots work well with raspberries, strawberries, clementines and blood oranges if you'd like some fruit on the side.

SERVES 4

1 Earl Grey tea bag

300g silken tofu

100g dark chocolate
(minimum 70%)

70ml maple syrup

1 teaspoon vanilla paste, or the
seeds from 1 vanilla pod

50g dark chocolate for grating
(optional)

a pinch of sea salt (optional)

Fill and boil a kettle and get all your ingredients together. Pour 100ml of boiling water over the tea bag and leave to steep.

Put the tofu inside a clean tea towel or cloth and wring out as much moisture as you can.

Put a pan on a low heat and add about 2cm of boiling water from the kettle. Place a heatproof bowl over the pan, add the chocolate and maple syrup and leave to melt.

Put the drained tofu into a food processor. Remove the tea bag from the tea and discard, then add the tea to the processor with the vanilla. Blend until smooth, then add the melted chocolate mixture and blend again until really smooth and silky.

Spoon the mixture into four little pots and place in the fridge to firm up a little. When you are ready to serve, top with a grating of chocolate and a pinch of sea salt, if you like.

Banana, date and candied pecan ice cream

A fast and healthy ice cream. Granted, this does require you to have some frozen bananas in your freezer, but I always freeze any over-ripe ones for ice creams and smoothies. Be sure to peel and roughly chop your bananas before you freeze them.

The pecan topping elevates this quick ice cream to another level of deliciousness, adding crunch, texture and some natural sweetness from the pecans and maple. It makes a super-quick and simple topping for shop-bought ice cream too.

....

Get all your ingredients together and put four bowls or glasses into the freezer to cool. Line a heatproof plate or bowl with a piece of greaseproof paper.

First, make your candied pecans. Heat a frying pan on a medium heat, then chop the pecans roughly and add to the pan to toast a little. Once the nuts have started to brown and are smelling great, add the maple syrup and continue to cook for a further minute. Transfer to your paper-lined heatproof plate or bowl, taking care not to touch the pecans, as the sugar will be really hot.

Put the frozen bananas into the bowl of a food processor with all the other ice cream ingredients. Blitz on high for 3–5 minutes, depending on how powerful your blender is, until you have a smooth ice cream.

If you are not eating your ice cream right away, you can put it into the cold glasses and put them back into the freezer for up to half an hour – but not too much longer, otherwise it will set hard and won't be soft and scoopable.

SERVES 4

FOR THE PECANS
100g pecans
2 tablespoons maple syrup

FOR THE ICE CREAM
3 frozen bananas (see introduction)
5 medjool dates, pitted
1 teaspoon vanilla paste, or the seeds from ½ a vanilla pod
a good pinch of ground cinnamon
100g coconut cream, or the cream from the top of a can of coconut milk

Coconut, rhubarb and lime panna cotta

My all-time friend and kitchen babe Emily made these especially for me, as they have all my favourite things packed into a perky little pudding. A good vegetarian panna cotta is a hard thing to come by, but Emily has smashed the formula here. Just the right side of sweet rhubarb, hidden below barely set coconut, lime and vanilla custard. All vegan, dairy, refined sugar and, most importantly, gelatine free. You'll want to thank Em yourself, as this dessert will make your life better.

Agar agar is a clever natural setting agent, made from seaweed, that you can use just like gelatine. Make sure it's fully dissolved before you pour it into the puddings or you may get a grainy texture.

....

Get all your ingredients and equipment together.

Put the coconut milk, coconut water, lime zest, maple syrup, vanilla bean paste and agar agar into a small saucepan and set aside.

Finely slice the rhubarb and put it into a medium frying pan with a knob of coconut oil. Place over a medium heat, add the coconut sugar and cook until the rhubarb starts to break down a little. Add the juice of the lime and continue to cook for a further 6–8 minutes, or until you are left with a thick, almost jam-like consistency. Remove from the heat and leave to cool.

Place the pan of coconut mixture over a medium heat and bring to the boil, without stirring. Once it's boiling, turn down the heat and simmer for 6 minutes, or until the agar agar has dissolved completely.

Place 2 tablespoons of rhubarb in the bottom of four dariole moulds, coffee cups or small ceramic bowls. Pour the coconut mixture into a jug and slowly, so that you don't disturb the layer of rhubarb, pour it into your moulds. Chill in the fridge for at least 3 hours. When you're ready to serve, dip the bottom of each mould in boiling water and turn out onto plates.

SERVES 4

1 × 400ml tin of coconut milk
200ml coconut water
the zest and juice of 1 unwaxed lime
100ml maple syrup
1 teaspoon vanilla bean paste
1 heaped tablespoon agar agar
500g bright pink rhubarb
coconut oil
120g coconut sugar

Salted almond butter
chocolate bars

A friend said these were the nicest chocolate bars he had ever tasted and
if they were on sale in the shops he would buy one every day. I think I would
too. These little bars are a triumph.

They are packed with goodness and have just a little sweetness from the
honey and the dark chocolate. If you want to keep things really pure here
you could use raw honey and raw chocolate for maximum nourishment.

These bars keep really well for a few weeks in the fridge and freeze brilliantly,
so a sweet hit that's full of goodness is never too far away. I make a batch
of these every couple of weeks, though they have become a favourite in my
house so rarely last more than a few days.

Fill and boil a kettle and get all your ingredients together. Line a small
square tin or baking tray with baking parchment.

Put the almonds into the bowl of a food processor and blitz for 5 minutes,
until the nuts are beginning to turn into a soft butter. Add the honey
or agave syrup, the coconut oil, vanilla and a good pinch of salt and blitz
to combine. Add the desiccated coconut and blitz again until you have
a scruffy dough-like mixture.

MAKES 24 BARS

200g almonds
3 tablespoons runny honey
or agave syrup
2 tablespoons melted coconut oil
the seeds from 1 vanilla pod,
or 1 teaspoon good vanilla extract
150g unsweetened
desiccated coconut
200g dark chocolate (70%)

Tip the dough into the lined baking tray and use clean wet hands to even
it out into a square about 2cm thick.

Put the baking tray into the freezer for a couple of minutes. Break the
chocolate into a bowl that will comfortably sit on top of one of your
pans. Put the pan on the heat, add a couple of centimetres of boiling
water and bring to a gentle simmer. Place the bowl on top of the
pan and let the chocolate melt, making sure the bowl doesn't touch
the simmering water.

Take the almond mixture out of the freezer and cut it into 24 bars. I do this by making six vertical slices and four horizontal ones. Pop them back into the freezer to chill.

Once the chocolate has melted, take it off the heat and allow it to cool and thicken, stirring occasionally. Cooling the chocolate a little is important, so that the bars will be thickly coated.

Line a second baking tray with parchment. Take the frozen bars out of the fridge and dip them into the chocolate, using two forks to turn them, then lay them on the parchment. Once you have coated all the bars, put them into the fridge to set.

These bars can be stacked in a container and kept in the fridge for up to a month. They also freeze really well.

20 MINUTES

Honey and orange ricotta and baked figs

This is one of my favourite things to make for a quick, amazing dessert when I have friends round. It is speedy enough for a weeknight too.

Baking ricotta is the easiest thing in the world but people always seem amazed by it. Get good sheep's ricotta if you can.

This is a good way to use up figs that are a little green or out of season, as roasting sweetens them up. This also works well with plums, apricots or halved strawberries.

I serve this with some little toasts for scooping up the ricotta.

....

Preheat your oven to 200 °C/180 °C fan/gas 6 and get all your ingredients together. Line a baking tray with a sheet of greaseproof paper.

Turn the ricotta out on to the paper-lined tray and drizzle over the honey. Grate over the orange zest and scrape over the vanilla seeds.

Halve the figs and scatter around the ricotta, then squeeze over the juice of half the orange, drizzle over a little more honey and put into the oven to bake for 20 minutes.

Roughly chop the almonds and scatter over everything for the last 5 minutes.

Serve straight from the oven in the middle of the table. Any leftovers can be scooped on to warm toast the next day.

SERVES 4–6

1 × 250g pot of ricotta cheese
1 tablespoon runny honey
1 unwaxed orange
the seeds from 1 vanilla pod
6 fresh figs
50g almonds

Cranachan

A super simple and quick dessert that always reminds me of a brilliant Scottish chef I worked with called Pete. I am sure Pete would like me to douse this in whisky, and if that's your thing, do it, I'm sure it would be wonderful.

This is my lighter take on cranachan, a Scottish quartet of raspberries, oats, brown sugar or honey, and cream. I use yoghurt (often coconut milk yoghurt) instead of cream, and lovely Scottish honey. Toasting the oats gives a satisfying biscuity flavour. This could even be eaten for breakfast.

SERVES 2–4,
DEPENDING ON APPETITE

100g fresh or frozen raspberries

50g walnuts

2 tablespoons rolled oats

a pinch of ground cinnamon

a good grating of fresh nutmeg

2 tablespoons runny honey

8 tablespoons good Greek yoghurt or coconut yoghurt

1 tablespoon bee pollen (optional)

Get all your ingredients together and put a frying pan on a medium heat. If using frozen raspberries, get them out now so they soften slightly. Roughly chop the walnuts, put them into the frying pan along with the oats and toast for a couple of minutes, until the oats are starting to turn golden. Take off the heat, add the cinnamon and nutmeg and 1 tablespoon of the honey.

Crush half the raspberries with a fork and fold them into the yoghurt, then stir in a bit more honey. Add the remaining whole raspberries, then fold in the toasted oatmeal and spoon into little glasses or bowls. If you like, you can sprinkle a little bee pollen over the top of each. Dainty and amazingly good for you.

quick fruit desserts

I have a sweet tooth and I like to finish my meal with something delicious and a little sweet, but goodness-packed too. Sometimes it's a snap of dark chocolate but other times it's a quick fruit pudding. Here are some ideas for fruit puddings that are all ready in less than 10 minutes.

QUICK FRUIT AND YOGHURT

Use your favourite yoghurt
(mine's coconut)

STRAWBERRIES, PISTACHIOS,
ORANGE ZEST

•

PAPAYA, LIME, DESICCATED COCONUT

•

RASPBERRIES, ROSE WATER,
TOASTED HAZELNUTS

•

DATES, PISTACHIOS, ORANGE,
ORANGE BLOSSOM WATER

•

APRICOTS, PEACHES, LEMON,
VANILLA, TOASTED ALMONDS

QUICK FRUIT SALADS

5 favourite combinations

WATERMELON, CHERRIES,
GRAPES, RASPBERRIES

•

PERSIMMON, MANGO, LIME,
BLOOD ORANGE

•

APPLES, PEARS, PLUMS,
BLACKBERRIES

•

STRAWBERRIES, LEMON,
VANILLA, PEACHES

•

MANGO, LIME, MINT,
PAPAYA, MELON

QUICK WARM FRUIT

Warm your fruit under the grill
or quickly in a pan

PRUNES, ARMAGNAC, VANILLA
(WARMED IN PAN)

•

PAPAYA, LIME ZEST (UNDER GRILL)

•

STRAWBERRIES, RHUBARB, MAPLE
SYRUP (WARMED IN PAN)

•

APRICOTS, HONEY, VANILLA
(UNDER GRILL)

•

PLUMS, CINNAMON, HONEY
(UNDER GRILL)

QUICK FRUIT ICE CREAM

Make instant ice cream by blitzing up
frozen fruit – try these for starters

FROZEN BANANA, HONEY

•

FROZEN BERRIES, VANILLA

•

FROZEN RASPBERRIES, LEMON

•

FROZEN PINEAPPLE, LIME

•

FROZEN WATERMELON = SORBET

QUICK
CHOCOLATE SAUCE

to accompany the ice creams

100G
MELTED CHOCOLATE

+

2 TABLESPOONS
MAPLE SYRUP

Dark chocolate goodness cookies

These are chewy, deeply chocolatey cookies. The kind that are so pleasingly dense, gooey and satisfying that even the greediest cookie eater can only manage a couple.

They aren't run-of-the-mill cookies, though. They're made from one of my favourite ingredients, though not one you might associate with baking – black beans. The fudgy, slightly sweet character of black beans works so well in baking, and of the numerous people I have asked to guess what is in these, so far no one has picked them out.

I have kept the double chocolate pretty pure here, but you could easily add some lemon or orange zest, raisins or sour cherries. For a more traditional chocolate chip cookie you can swap the black beans for cannellini beans.

Oh, and did I mention these are naturally free of gluten, dairy and refined sugar? Almost Virtuous Deliciousness.

....

Preheat your oven to 210°C/190°C/gas 7. Get all your ingredients together and line a baking tray with greaseproof paper.

If you are using chia seeds, mix them with 4 tablespoons of cold water. Mix the chia mixture or the eggs, maple syrup and vanilla in a bowl and set aside.

Drain your beans, rinse well under cold water, then put them into a food processor with the coconut oil, cocoa and salt and blend until you have a smooth dough.

Add the maple syrup mixture and pulse until you have a wet dough. The batter will be quite liquid, but will still hold together.

MAKES ABOUT 10 COOKIES

2 tablespoons chia seeds, or 2 free-range or organic eggs

125ml maple syrup

1 teaspoon vanilla extract

1 × 400g tin of black beans

2 tablespoons coconut oil

40g cocoa powder

a good pinch of flaky sea salt, plus more for sprinkling

75g dark chocolate (70%)

50g medjool dates

Scoop the whole lot out into a bowl. Chop the chocolate and the dates and stir into the dough.

Spoon a generous tablespoon of the batter on to the lined baking sheet and use the back of the spoon to flatten the top to a cookie shape, as they will not spread very much when baked. Sprinkle the tops with a little salt and bake for 12–15 minutes, until the edges are browning.

Honey, almond and basil cheesecake

This is my super-quick version of the cheesecake that has been raved about, from a London restaurant called Honey and Co. Theirs is much posher and more complicated. Mine takes 10 minutes. We are meeting in the middle.

I use shredded wheat here, which you might think sounds rather weird, but it is my attempt at quickly mimicking the brilliant shards of kadaif pastry that sit below the strained feta at Honey and Co. I think it works pretty well.

Shredded wheat is one of the last true cereals, and when I was growing up it was what my dad ate for breakfast every morning. Unlike most cereals it has no additives, and you can buy organic versions in health food shops too. I often use soft feta cheese here, which I can buy easily in my local shop, but ricotta will work just as well if soft feta is not easy for you to come by.

Get all your ingredients together.

Put a pan on a medium heat and, once hot, add the almonds and cook for a minute or two until they smell toasty. Put into a bowl for later.

Put the pan back on the heat, add 3 tablespoons of honey and crumble in the shredded wheat. Heat for a couple of minutes, tossing all the time to coat the shredded wheat with the honey. Take off the heat.

Whip the ricotta or feta in a bowl with the vanilla, the final tablespoon of honey and the zest of half the lemon, using a hand-held electric whisk or a balloon whisk and some determination, until smooth, whipped and cloudy. If you are using it, stir in the orange blossom water. Roughly chop the cooled almonds.

Divide the honey-glazed shreds between plates and top with a generous spoonful of the ricotta. Scatter over the berries and almonds and some torn mint or basil, and drizzle with a little more honey, if you like.

SERVES 4

a handful of skinned almonds

4 tablespoons runny honey, plus more for drizzling

2 shredded wheat

250g good ricotta or soft Greek feta cheese

1 tablespoon vanilla paste

1 unwaxed lemon

a dash of orange blossom water (optional)

a couple of handfuls of seasonal berries

a few sprigs of fresh mint or basil

Pistachio and raspberry brownies

These brownies are for my mum and dad. They love life and are the two best people I know. They are also, in the nicest possible way, chalk and cheese, so finding things they both love can be hard, and this is where these pretty perfect brownies come in. My dad loves chocolate; my mum loves raspberries and pistachios. Here all the things they love come together in a ridiculously delicious harmony.

These dense, gooey and chocolatey brownies are made with ground almonds and coconut sugar, so they are a little lighter and more nutrient-packed than your average brownie. I almost always make these with chia seeds in place of the eggs, which makes them vegan too. If you use chia seeds you'll need to add a little baking powder to make sure the brownies rise.

Frozen raspberries work really well here, and in the summer I sometimes make these with pitted halved cherries too. If coconut sugar is a bridge too far then soft brown sugar will work too.

....

Preheat the oven to 180°C/fan 160°C/gas 4 and get all your ingredients and equipment together. Grease a small brownie tin with coconut oil or butter and line it with baking paper (mine is 20cm × 20cm but anything around that size will do).

If you are using chia seeds rather than eggs, put the seeds into a little bowl and add 9 tablespoons of cold water. Leave to form a gel-like paste.

Place a heatproof bowl over a pan of gently simmering water, making sure the bowl doesn't touch the water. Put 150g of the chocolate into the bowl with the coconut oil or butter and let them melt, stirring from time to time. Once melted, take the bowl off the heat and stir in the sugar, followed by the beaten eggs, one by one, or the chia seed mixture, and finally the vanilla and ground almonds and the baking powder, if using, plus half

MAKES 12 BROWNIES

3 organic or free-range eggs, beaten, or 3 tablespoons chia seeds

200g dark chocolate (70%)

150g coconut oil or unsalted butter

250g coconut sugar

1 teaspoon natural vanilla extract, or the seeds from 1 vanilla pod

150g ground almonds

1 heaped teaspoon baking powder (if you are using chia seeds, not eggs)

125g raspberries (frozen or fresh)

50g pistachio nuts

the raspberries (if they are frozen don't defrost them first) and half the pistachios. Roughly chop the remaining 50g of chocolate and fold through the mixture too.

Pour the brownie mix into the lined tin and scatter over the rest of the raspberries and the pistachios. Bake for 25–30 minutes, until just cooked but still a little soft in the middle.

Leave to cool for at least 20 minutes before cutting. These will keep for 3–4 days but I challenge you to make them last that long!

Instant raw salted caramel chocolate mousse

I am not one of those healthy eaters who likes things to taste worthy, so don't be put off when you read the virtuous ingredient list for this dessert. I want chocolate to be rich, indulgent and moreish.

It's a recipe I feel a bit embarrassed writing down, as it is so, so simple, but often those are the best.

A powerful blender works best here, but failing that, a hand blender and a bit of elbow grease will do just fine. For best results, make sure your banana is frozen and your avocado and lemon are fridge cold. And be sure not to use a really large banana, or the flavour of banana will be overpowering.

I have left the serving size a little ambiguous – this is rich, so some might like a dainty cupful while real chocolate lovers might like a bit more. It's easily doubled or even tripled for parties and keeps well in the fridge for a few hours.

SERVES 2–4

FOR THE MOUSSE
1 ripe avocado
1 small frozen banana
juice of ½ a lemon or lime
3 tablespoons cocoa powder
(I use the raw stuff)
2 tablespoons maple syrup

FOR THE SALTED
CARAMEL SAUCE
6 medjool dates
2 tablespoons maple syrup
a good pinch of sea salt

Get all your ingredients together. Put all the mousse ingredients into a blender with a tablespoon of cold water and blitz on high until everything is whipped to a smooth mousse, stopping to scrape down the sides a couple of times – this may take a couple of minutes in a less powerful blender. Scoop it out into cups and give the blender a quick rinse.

Put the de-stoned dates into the blender (if your blender is large, a hand-held blender might work better here) with the maple syrup, a tablespoon of cold water and a good pinch of sea salt. Blend until you have a thick, smooth caramel sauce. Drizzle the sauce on top of the mousse and top with some extra salt crystals.

Index

The following recipes are vegan or gluten-free, or require only simple tweaking to adapt them.

Acknowledgements

This book, in keeping with its theme, came together in quite a short time. This was made more joyful and much less stressful by the amazing group of people I feel lucky enough to call my family and friends.

Firstly to John 'Ideas Man' Dale, your belief in me is unwavering, and your constant, gentle support is all I could ever wish for. You know how much of this belongs to you. I can't wait to marry you on the island and for our next adventure.

To Mum and Dad, the kindness, love and support you continue to send my way leaves me lost for words. The freedom and belief you've afforded and instilled in me has meant I have been free to follow my own path, and to me that is the greatest gift you could have given. You are truly my two favourite people.

To Laura, my sister, I look to you for everything, and always have, thank you for striving to be the best you can be in every way and in doing so bringing me along with you. Thank you too for so generously sharing all your food discoveries and ideas, many of which fill the pages of this book.

To Owen, my brother, the youngest, but also somehow the wisest in our family, you are a true individual, a kind soul, a trail blazer. You are led by what's right and if more people in the world were like you we'd be a lot better off. I am really proud of you.

To Emily, your help making this book what it is went above and beyond – helping me out when inspiration was lacking and keeping me going when the task seemed insurmountable. You are a truly incredible, generous and brilliantly creative soul. This book would not have been written without you. Thank you.

To Louise Haines, I am humbled by your belief in me and my cooking, thank you for caring so much about every detail of this book, working with you in your brilliant organic way is a joy, I feel very lucky to be published by you and 4th Estate.

To Georgia Mason, the most wonderful editor, in the shortest of timescales you have held this book together, as if it was your own, which in part it undoubtedly is. I am so grateful for every single thing you have done to make me as proud of this book as I am.

Thank you too to Annie Lee for your close eye, and to Morwenna Loughman for all your help.

To Matt Russell, you have made this book come alive. Again under tight timelines you put everything into this, at the same time as leaving your ego at the door, it's a rare and generous skill. I think your photographs are just brilliant. Thank you. To Ollie, Matt's assistant, thank you for your island charm, the shoots were so much better for your presence.

To Sandra who designed this book with such grace, thank you, you have worked stupidly hard to make this the book it is. I am in awe of your dedication and creativity. I can't tell you how much it means to know you care as much as I do. Thank you.

To Michelle Kane thank you in advance for the amazing things I know you have up your sleeve. Thanks too to all the papers, magazines and blogs who allowed me to grace their pages, especially Allan Jenkins and the team at OFM.

To Jess, thank you for everything, for taking it all so brilliantly in your stride, you are a rare combination of shining creativity and amazing pragmatism. I feel very lucky to have you around.

To Alex Gray, thanks for all your hard work in the kitchen, your amazing lunches, you are a true gentleman.

To amazing friends who helped test the recipes in this book, you are incredible, thank you. Your notes, comments and feedback give me such confidence in the recipes in this book and I am so grateful for every single meal you cooked. Krys Gaffney, Ceri Tallett, James Bannochie and Emma Ballinger, James Gold, Angelique Mercier, Jon and Laura Plane, Anna and Ellen Fermie, Olenka Lawrenson, Emily Taylor, Bryony Walker, Sian Dale, Sian Tallett, Danny McCubbin, Anja Forrest Dunk, Mimi Beaven, Mersedeh Prewer, Lizzie Winn, Priya Thakar, Eileen Power, Ella Power, Alice Power, Philippa Spence, Christina Mackenzie, Alex Grimes, Carys Williams, Nick and Anna Probert, Kris Hallenga, Luke Shaller.

Some amazing friends have helped this books on its way. To Ceri Tallett, the best in the business, thank you for your eye, your words and your generosity, which is actually endless. Now it's your turn. I want a Tallett on my bookshelf. To Liz, you have skills I wish I had, thanks for sharing them with me, and keeping me on track. You are gold. To Crystal, my cousin, an all-in-one Anna Jones PR machine. You are unstoppable, thanks for all your help.

To Brickett Davda, The Conran Shop, David Mellor and Labour and Wait. Thank you all for trusting me with your insanely beautiful things. I pretended they were mine for a few weeks, it was hard to give them back. You are all incredibly generous.

To all my friends who for the last six months haven't heard a peep out of me, this book is the reason why. I love you all and look forward to a summer filled with your faces.

And lastly but most importantly every single person who brought a copy of *A Modern Way to Eat*, to each person who cooked a recipe, to everyone who looked at my blog. You all inspire me everyday, I love reading your emails and seeing the pictures of things you have made, it still blows me away every time. I am so thankful that we are all on this journey together. You are all amazing.